How to RESCUE a RUIN

by setting up a local Buildings Preservation Trust

Hilary Weir

Front cover — *Rutherglen, a Grade II* listed mid-18th century house at the apex of Church Street and Church Lane in Ledbury, Herefordshire, in 1986. It is part of a complex of listed buildings which was under threat of demolition for nearly 30 years.*

Back cover — *Rutherglen in 1988, after rehabilitation by the County of Hereford & Worcester Building Preservation Trust. The Architectural Heritage Fund helped the Trust finance the £420,000 restoration of Rutherglen and three other buildings by lending £100,000 at its standard rate of 5% per annum.*

Figure 1 — *Nos. 5-8 Market Street, Bradford-on-Avon, Wiltshire, in 1980 — four listed buildings in critical condition.*

Figure 2 — *The same buildings in 1982. Bradford-on-Avon Preservation Trust restored them as shops with maisonettes above, a £211,000 project which the AHF assisted with a loan of £60,000 in 1981.*

How to RESCUE a RUIN

by setting up a local Buildings Preservation Trust

Hilary Weir

The
Architectural
Heritage
Fund

THIS BOOK HAS BEEN PRODUCED WITH FINANCIAL ASSISTANCE
FROM THE DEPARTMENT OF THE ENVIRONMENT

How to Rescue a Ruin
is published by

a registered charity (No. 266780)
established in 1976
to help Buildings Preservation Trusts
finance preservation projects

Copies of this and other AHF publications are available from:

The Architectural Heritage Fund
17 Carlton House Terrace, London SW1Y 5AW
Telephone: 01-925 0199
Fax: 01-321 0180

Published in December 1989
© The Architectural Heritage Fund

ISBN 0 9515468 0 5

Chapter Seven by **Rosemary Watt**
Drawings by **Richard Just**
Design and most photography by **Victor Rose**

Extracts from the *Directory of Public Sources of Grants
for the Repair and Conversion of Historic Buildings*
reproduced by kind permission of English Heritage.

Printed on recycled paper by Chandlers (Printers) Ltd,
Saxon Mews, Reginald Road, Bexhill-on-Sea,
East Sussex

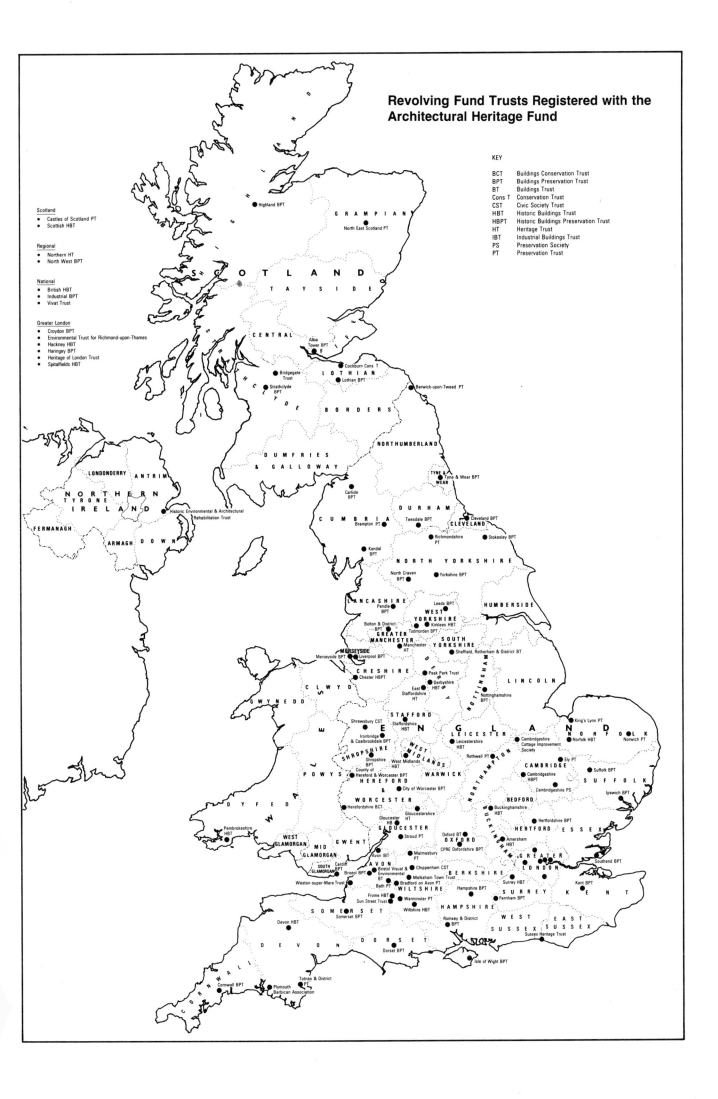

Revolving Fund Trusts Registered with the Architectural Heritage Fund

KEY

BCT	Buildings Conservation Trust
BPT	Buildings Preservation Trust
BT	Buildings Trust
Cons T	Conservation Trust
CST	Civic Society Trust
HBT	Historic Buildings Trust
HBPT	Historic Buildings Preservation Trust
HT	Heritage Trust
IBT	Industrial Buildings Trust
PS	Preservation Society
PT	Preservation Trust

Scotland
- Castles of Scotland PT
- Scottish HBT

Regional
- Northern HT
- North West BPT

National
- British HBT
- Industrial BPT
- Vivat Trust

Greater London
- Croydon BPT
- Environmental Trust for Richmond-upon-Thames
- Hackney HBT
- Haringey BPT
- Heritage of London Trust
- Spitalfields HBT

Contents

Figure 3 — *Chippenham Civic Society Trust took the opportunity to advertise its rehabilitation of 37 The Causeway, one of the last burgage houses in Chippenham, Wiltshire. The AHF loaned £70,000 of the £140,000 required.*

Figure 4 — *The County of Hereford & Worcester BPT appealing for help with its Ledbury project in 1987 (see also front and back cover captions).*

Preface

This short book is aimed at everyone who cares about the buildings in which we live, work and play. It is a practical handbook, intended to give people who would like to "do something" step by step advice about setting up a buildings preservation trust and tackling their first project. Anyone wishing for additional guidance or information should get in touch, by letter or telephone, with the Architectural Heritage Fund.

The present book takes its lead from the Civic Trust's seminal 1972 report to the Department of the Environment, *Forming a Buildings Preservation Trust,* which has been out of print for more than ten years. It also draws upon *Building Preservation Trusts — A Challenge For Scotland,* published in 1984 by the Architectural Heritage Society of Scotland (then the Scottish Georgian Society), which remains the essential work of reference for anyone setting up a trust north of the border (see Bibliography for details).

In preparing a new publication on how to set up a buildings preservation trust, it has been possible to take into account the Architectural Heritage Fund's 13 years of day-to-day involvement with buildings preservation trusts in every part of the United Kingdom, and to consult a number of people currently working in the field. This book therefore looks at the background to the buildings preservation trust movement and the scope for expansion, discusses the legal framework, formalities and practical steps to be taken when establishing a trust, outlines the management of a first project, and offers some introductory advice about Value Added Tax and fund raising.

I am grateful to many people who read the manuscript and made helpful comments, in particular Vanessa Brand of English Heritage, Geoffrey Goldsmith of HM Customs & Excise, Barry Joyce of Derbyshire County Council, Bob Kindred of Ipswich Borough Council, Geoffrey Hayhurst and Martin Paisner of Paisner & Co (Honorary Solicitors to the Architectural Heritage Fund), Mark Seymour of the Charity Commission, and Roger Wools of the Alex Gordon Partnership (Architects and Project Managers). Hard-pressed officers of buildings preservation trusts in every part of the United Kingdom also made time to go through the draft and suggest improvements. Lastly I must thank my colleague Rosemary Watt, who contributed the chapter on VAT and commented on the rest of the text at various stages of its evolution.

Hilary Weir
The Architectural Heritage Fund

December 1989

There are few more disheartening sights than an old building, boarded up, slates slipping from the roof, buddleia sprouting from drain pipes, walls daubed with graffiti, unlovely and obviously unloved. It is a sight which provokes incredulity, indignation, even anger. Why has such a building — which could be providing much-needed housing, shop or working accommodation — fallen into disuse, been allowed to deteriorate, to become an eyesore instead of an attractive feature of the street or neighbourhood? What can be done to put it back into commission?

Most people, however indignant, pass by on the other side of the road, preferring to leave it to others to "do something" about the problem. The local civic or amenity society might decide to protest to the District Council. One or two individuals might make an effort to discover who owns the building, only to recoil when confronted by the financial, legal and administrative implications of seeking to acquire and restore it. But unless protest is accompanied by a viable proposal for rehabilitation, the building is likely to remain derelict until the owner is able to realise its value, more often than not by selling the freehold for radical redevelopment.

The most practicable alternative to wringing one's hands while a historic building decays is for the local buildings preservation trust to step in, buy the freehold, undertake a high-quality restoration with the aid of grant and low-interest loan finance, and sell or lease the refurbished building on the open market. If there is no preservation trust in the area, then it only takes two or three people who care enough about the fate of historic buildings in their town to set one up.

What are buildings preservation trusts?

Buildings preservation trusts (BPTs for short) are voluntary organisations, set up by like-minded individuals who are willing to devote time and effort, without pay or other financial reward, to a good cause. They exist principally in order to save high risk, low return historic buildings in which nobody else is prepared to invest. Not the major monuments, whose long-term preservation is of national concern and may require continual subsidy, but more local, everyday buildings which are able to earn their keep once repaired and rehabilitated.

BPTs have a number of advantages over both the private sector and local government.

Because they have charitable status, BPTs can raise and co-ordinate various forms of finance.

— **grants** from central and local government;

— **low-interest loans** from the Architectural Heritage Fund;

— **donations, gifts in kind and concessionary loans** from companies, charitable trusts and the public at large.

Because their principal motive is preservation, BPTs are unlikely to cut architectural corners in the interests of a quick profit.

Because almost all BPTs are set up as limited liability companies, with powers to enter into legal contracts, to buy and sell property, and to borrow money, they can mobilise quickly when a threat is brought to their attention.

And because most BPTs are formed by members of the community and operate within a relatively small geographical area, they are able to enlist popular support, not only for their efforts to achieve publicity, raise funds and bring pressure to bear — on owners, local authority planning departments and others whose co-operation is required — but often too in the search for the human skills and building materials necessary to accomplish each project.

Figure 5 — *Desperately needing attention: the unusual groin-vaulted interior of the Grade A listed Stables at Cromarty House in Cromarty, Ross & Cromarty. The AHF loaned Cromarty Arts Trust £80,000 in 1989 towards the cost of preserving and converting the Stables into studios and workshops.*

The size of the challenge

It might be thought that the "heritage" boom of the 1980s, reinforced by heightened popular concern about environmental issues in general, would have put the "demolish and redevelop" school out of fashion, if not of business. Old buildings, expertly restored and sensitively converted to modern needs, are popular with those who use them. They make a unique contribution not only to the character of the local environment, but also to its vitality, by augmenting and upgrading its residential and commercial accommodation, its industrial, leisure and tourist facilities.

But although the case for preservation is now both widely accepted and underpinned by legislation, the money, skills and initiative required to rescue buildings from redundancy and dereliction are still too thinly spread. Figures collected by English Heritage, for example, suggest that as many as 25,000 listed buildings, as well as a very large number of unlisted buildings in conservation areas[1], are threatened by

neglect, and that more than one building of architectural or historic interest is actually lost *each day*. The size of the problem is such that in 1988 English Heritage launched a "Buildings at Risk" campaign, in order to gather and collate information about such buildings and — by providing grant aid for the purpose — to encourage owners and local authorities to carry out emergency repairs (for details, see Appendix C).

Buildings at risk

It is seldom difficult, at local level, to identify "problem" buildings which are at risk: textile mills, churches, public baths, schools or railway stations, for example, made redundant by changes in technology, demography, economic patterns and popular taste, are threatened by dereliction. A newer, though perhaps less immediately obvious challenge is posed by traditional high street shops, many of whose upper floors are unused and poorly maintained, putting the whole property at risk. And there remains, throughout the country, a great deal of down-at-heel Victorian and earlier housing. Market forces will ensure that some of these buildings are saved, but others pose problems so complex that few private owners are willing or able to make the investment required to give them a new lease of life. It is precisely here that BPTs can and should step in.

[1] The Secretary of State for the Environment in England, and the Secretaries of State for Scotland and Northern Ireland, are required to compile lists of buildings of special architectural or historic interest for the guidance of local planning authorities. See Appendix B for details.

Figure 6 — *Within 10 minutes of central Manchester, this Grade II listed Georgian stable block in the grounds of Nazareth House in Prestwich was severely derelict in 1987.*

Figure 7 — *North West BPT transformed the stables into 10 residential units with the aid of a £150,000 loan from the AHF in 1988 (see p. 13).*

Revolving funds and single project trusts

There are two principal types of buildings preservation trust: those formed to save more than one building, which will be referred to as **revolving fund trusts,** and those formed to save a particular building, which will be referred to as **single project trusts.** This book is chiefly concerned with revolving fund trusts, but much of the information about such trusts is also relevant to the formation and work of single project trusts.

First beginnings

BPTs are not a recent phenomenon. The oldest on the Architectural Heritage Fund's Register, the Cambridgeshire Preservation Society, was founded in 1929.[1] But the concept was initially slow to spread, perhaps partly because many of the early trusts retained and managed the buildings they restored and so could not recycle their working capital as quickly as the later generation of revolving fund trusts. Whatever the reasons, between 1929 and 1970 only a score of trusts was formed, and their work was little known or understood.

The growth of the movement

The potential of BPTs was recognised in the late 1960s by the Civic Trust, which concluded (in a 1971 report to the Department of the Environment) that a national network of something like 200 trusts, between them handling about 400 buildings a year, could make a significant impact on buildings at risk. To bridge the gap between what trusts could raise themselves and the finance required for their projects, the Civic Trust recommended an initiative by the Government to create a National Buildings Conservation Fund with a capital of £1 million.

A national fund

The Government endorsed the Civic Trust's view, and in July 1974, as part of the UK campaign for European Architectural Heritage Year 1975, made a commitment to match, up to a maximum of £500,000, whatever could be raised from the private sector for a national revolving fund. An appeal was launched, and in 1976 The Architectural Heritage Fund (AHF) opened for

business with a potential capital of £1 million and a mandate to provide preservation trusts with loan finance at a concessionary rate. The existence of a national source of cheap working capital did much to stimulate the formation of revolving fund trusts, whose number quintupled between 1975 and 1989.

What have BPTs achieved?

A number of BPTs are extremely active, tackling project after project — often with the aid of AHF loans — and keeping their capital hard at work. Very often, a trust will have the satisfaction of knowing that a project has repercussions well beyond the preservation of a particular building, in that a successful rehabilitation has the effect of boosting local confidence and stimulating an inflow of private sector money to nearby properties. The BPT has thus been the catalyst for wider regeneration of the area.

Individually, BPT projects vary greatly in scale, complexity and cost.

> At one end of the spectrum is something as modest and straightforward as the restoration and upgrading of a small property in a terrace of weavers' cottages in Barnard Castle, County Durham (fig. 8), which cost Teesdale Buildings Preservation Trust some £14,000 in 1977.

> At the other is the highly ambitious rehabilitation by Derbyshire Historic Buildings Trust of 57 derelict railway workers' houses in Derby, at an overall cost — in 1980 — of some £1.25 million (figs. 30 and 31).

> In between, and involving more radical conversion, was the transformation in 1988 by North West Buildings Preservation Trust of a derelict Georgian stable block in Greater Manchester into ten small houses, a project whose cost was in the region of £425,000 (figs. 6 and 7).

In every case, the trusts concerned were able to sell the properties well enough to increase their working capital and move on without delay to other projects, demonstrating that BPTs can successfully rescue even the most difficult historic buildings from dereliction.

Architectural Heritage Fund loans

The upward curve in BPT activity is mirrored in the volume of the Architectural Heritage Fund's low-interest loans. In its first five years (from May 1976 to April 1981), the AHF loaned just under £1 million in support of 32 projects. By the end of its first decade, these totals had risen to more than £3 million for 84 projects. Less than three and a half years later, at the

---

[1]The Architectural Heritage Fund was established principally in order to support trusts constituted as revolving funds, and therefore does not register single project trusts. Many single project trusts have however received low-interest loans from the Architectural Heritage Fund. The Register of trusts is reproduced in Appendix F.

beginning of October 1989, the overall amount loaned since 1976 had grown to £8.7 million for 177 projects. The Architectural Heritage Fund has had to make strenuous efforts to augment its resources in order to keep pace with demand for loans, with the result that its capital increased from £1 million in 1981 to £4.6 million in 1989.

The need for more trusts

Although the growth in the number and activities of BPTs is encouraging, it has not been such as to enable the movement to make a major contribution, nationwide, to the preservation of threatened buildings. Information collected by the Architectural Heritage Fund in December 1988 revealed that between 1983 and 1988, revolving fund trusts together completed fewer than 230 preservation projects — a long way off the Civic Trust's 1971 target of 200 projects a year. Given the number of buildings at risk, it is imperative to bring about the formation of many more trusts in almost every part of the United Kingdom.

A flawed network

A glance at the map on p. 5 shows that the existing BPT network is not only very thin, but also contains gaping holes which the few "national" preservation trusts (British Historic Buildings Trust; Historic, Environmental and Architectural Rehabilitation Trust; Industrial Buildings Preservation Trust; Scottish Historic Buildings Trust; and Vivat Trust) cannot hope to fill. Most urban conurbations, for example, and a surprising number of counties, are badly served. In Bedfordshire, Berkshire, Lincolnshire, Humberside, Warwickshire, and most of Wales and Northern Ireland, there are no revolving fund trusts at all. Elsewhere — in Cheshire, Cumbria, Essex, Lancashire, Northumberland and Northamptonshire for example — there are one or two trusts, but these are based on particular towns: without a county-wide trust, or a much larger number of local trusts, the impact made on that county's threatened buildings must be minimal. The opposite is true in Bristol, and — most notably — in Wiltshire; but if towns like Bradford-on-Avon, Chippenham, Malmesbury, Melksham and Warminster can each support a revolving fund, why should not similar communities elsewhere?

Plugging the gaps

One reason why the BPT movement is not fulfilling its potential is the fact that trusts have not had access either to other trusts or to a central support system. As a result many have toiled in isolation, unwittingly reinventing the wheel and wrestling to overcome problems on which there is by now a substantial, but scattered and largely unprocessed, volume of knowledge. The AHF has always done its best to help and advise BPTs, both individually and through its biannual newsletter, *Preservation in Action*. But the AHF is based in London, exists to make cheap loans, and has no first-hand experience of managing preservation projects. It therefore very much welcomed the initiative taken by a number of BPTs in 1988, which led to the formation of a new national organisation, the Association of Preservation Trusts (APT), in 1989.

"APT"

APT is composed of nine "committees" or area groups of BPTs (six in England, one each in Scotland, Wales and Northern Ireland), and a central or UK committee composed of one representative of every area and three representatives of the AHF. BPTs are thus able to discuss problems and exchange views at area meetings and, through area representatives, to feed information and requests for assistance to the UK committee. Anyone interested in setting up a BPT should ask the AHF for the name and address of their area representative, who ought to be able to offer practical advice and do much to eliminate the feeling that a new trust must solve every problem on its own.

CHAPTER TWO

THE ANATOMY OF A BUILDINGS PRESERVATION TRUST

A many-headed beast

All BPTs, whether revolving fund or single project, are "voluntary" organisations, in the sense that they are set up by like-minded individuals coming together for a particular, non-profit-making purpose. Within this general classification, however, the size and shape of the many organisations known as buildings preservation trusts — BPTs — vary widely:

At one end of the spectrum, a BPT may be a very small, entirely local organisation composed of four or five individuals and formed to tackle a threatened building or buildings in the vicinity of a single town.

At the opposite end of the spectrum, a BPT may be established at the initiative of the local authority as a large organisation with an open membership and a mandate to operate throughout an entire county.

There are also:

— hybrid trusts, set up as joint ventures by members of the community and the local authority;
— trusts which operate county-wide but which have no formal links with local government;
— trusts which operate across county boundaries, encompassing a defined region or even the whole of Britain;
— local authority-inspired trusts which restrict their operations to a single town or municipality;
— trusts with a broad social and economic remit which includes preserving a historic building or buildings.

Revolving fund trusts

Whatever their origin or composition, all trusts referred to as **revolving fund trusts** are constituted to acquire, restore and — subject to suitable provisions for their future preservation and maintenance — dispose of properties deemed worthy of preservation, and to apply the proceeds of one project to the working capital required for the next. Revolving fund trusts should therefore be able to draw on any surplus from a financially successful project in order to tackle a particularly difficult building or buildings, whose rehabilitation is bound to cost more than the income received from grant and sale.

Some revolving fund trusts also undertake projects which involve retaining and managing buildings once restored. This however ties up a high proportion of their working capital to the detriment of further projects, and by far the majority of revolving fund trusts concentrate on projects which involve acquisition, rehabilitation and disposal.

Single project trusts

Trusts referred to as **single project trusts** are usually set up because of concern within the community about a particular property or group of properties whose future cannot be secured within the cash limits,

Figure 8 — *Teesdale BPT cut its teeth by rehabilitating the left hand section of this 18th century weavers' cottage in Thorngate, Barnard Castle, Co Durham, in 1977 (see p. 13). The AHF loaned £4,000.*

Figure 9 — *No. 33 Thorngate in 1978, after restoration. The Trust subsequently tackled the building next door, and later a property further down the same street. See also figs. 16 and 17.*

timetable or open market framework of a buy, restore and sell approach, and for which there is a viable community use. The majority of single project trusts therefore undertake not only the rehabilitation of the property, but also its subsequent care and management. This kind of trust is likely to retain ownership and to be closely involved in running a venture compatible with the character and physiognomy of the building and capable in the longer term of generating sufficient finance to enable it to pay its way. A minority however may sell the building once it has been preserved.

The legal framework

Both revolving fund and single project preservation trusts are voluntary organisations. But their business involves buying, restoring, selling and/or managing property, for which it is necessary to mobilise large amounts of money. In order to protect the people who take decisions from being held personally responsible if the trust stumbles into debt or encounters other legal problems, it is advisable for the organisation to have an existence or identity of its own, separate from its individual members.

There are various ways of giving an organisation its own identity, but the most appropriate is **incorporation as a company limited by guarantee.** In order to have the advantages of charitable status, BPTs formed as companies limited by guarantee in England and Wales should also register with the Charity Commission; in Scotland, they should apply to the Inland Revenue for charitable status; and in Northern Ireland to the Department of Commerce.

The advantages of incorporation

The principal advantage of forming a company limited by guarantee is that the BPT acquires a distinct legal identity. Provided due care is exercised in the administration, the liability of individual members is limited: in the event that the trust has to be wound up, members will be called upon to contribute only a nominal sum (usually not more than £5) towards its debts. This enables the trust to enter into business transactions of

a magnitude which the trustees of an unincorporated association, who have ultimate personal responsibility for its debts, might be reluctant to risk.

An incorporated trust also has clearly defined powers which facilitate its business operations. Among those normally spelled out in its "constitution" are the powers to buy, sell, lease or own property, to raise funds, to enter into contracts, to invest, and to borrow money against the security of the trust's assets. All are essential for the efficient conduct of BPT business.

It is advisable for anyone interested in setting up a BPT to take the trouble to become acquainted with the legal framework within which the trust will operate (see Chapter Three). Because the majority of BPTs are incorporated as limited liability companies, this book does not go into the formalities of constituting a BPT as a charitable trust with a Trust Deed or Declaration of Trust, nor those for registering as an Industrial and Provident Society. One or two very active revolving fund trusts are constituted in this way.

Figure 10 — *Yorkshire Buildings Preservation Trust's discreet commemorative plaque in Front Street, Acomb, North Yorkshire.*

Every buildings preservation trust needs a "constitution" setting out first its objectives and powers, and second its rules and procedures. This chapter concentrates on the formalities involved in establishing a trust as a company limited by guarantee and registered as a charity (the form recommended in Chapter Two), and the responsibilities of those who become members and/or "directors". It should be read in conjunction with Chapter Four, which describes the practical steps that need to be taken to set up a trust within this framework.

Much of what follows is not applicable to Scotland, where there is no equivalent of the Charity Commission. People interested in forming a BPT in Scotland should therefore obtain a copy of the Architectural Heritage Society of Scotland's booklet, *Buildings Preservation Trusts — A Challenge for Scotland.*[1] Northern Irish legislation is closely based on that in England, but there are a number of variants. Advice should be sought from the Department of Commerce.[2]

The "constitution" of a buildings preservation trust

The "constitution" of every limited liability company takes the form of a Memorandum and Articles of Association. These are formal instruments governing the aims, activities, structure and responsibilities of the BPT. Its operations will be subject both to the provisions of the Companies Acts, and to the general law relating to charities.

Model Governing Instrument (Memorandum and Articles of Association)

The Architectural Heritage Fund has published a *Model* Memorandum and Articles of Association in order to reduce the paper work and thus the cost involved in setting up a local revolving fund.[3] This has been approved by the Charity Commission, and anyone proposing to set up a BPT in England or Wales who follows the *Model* closely should be able to register with a minimum of formality, both as a limited liability company with the Department of Trade and Industry, and as a charity with the Charity Commission.

Figure 11 — *Derbyshire Historic Buildings Trust staked its claim on Railway Cottages well before work began (see also p. 13 and figs. 25, 30 and 31).*

The trust's "objects"

The first requirement when setting up a revolving fund trust is to decide what the trust intends to do, in other words to agree upon what the Memorandum of Association will refer to as its **"object"**. In order to qualify for charitable status, *all* the trust's objects must be charitable, and *all* its activities must directly further those charitable objects. If the trust wishes to engage in additional activities which support the trust (eg by raising money) but which might not themselves be charitable, it will have to set up a separate trading company which will covenant its income to the trust. The trading company can be a wholly-owned subsidiary, whose directors, members and staff (if any) are identical to those of the BPT.

What is charitable and what is not is determined by charity law. (Free booklets on this subject are available from the Charity Commission.) The easiest way to be sure that the objects proposed for a buildings preservation trust are charitable will be to use the wording in the AHF Model. The essential ingredient is **"preservation"** — of buildings, monuments, etc — **"for the benefit of"** the people of a named town or area, and/or "the public generally", depending on the chosen area of operation. Other objects can include conserving and/or promoting the protection and conservation of "the character and heritage" of the cities, towns and villages in the area of operation; and advancing public education and interest in the history of the area.

---

[1]The Architectural Heritage Society of Scotland, 43b Manor Place, Edinburgh EH3 7EB (telephone 031-225 9724).

[2]Department of Commerce, 43-47 Chichester Street, Belfast BT1 4RJ.

[3]*Model Governing Instrument for a Local Buildings Preservation Trust,* available from The Architectural Heritage Fund, 17 Carlton House Terrace, London SW1Y 5AW (telephone 01-925 0199). See also Appendix D.

The trust's "beneficial area"

A trust may pursue its "objects" only within the **beneficial area** defined in its Memorandum. When deciding the trust's objects, it is therefore necessary to consider the geographical range within which the trust is to operate.

It is important to be both clear and far sighted about this. There are legal limitations on the alteration of a trust's objects, and trustees (members of the trust's management committee, by whatever name it is, and they are, known) are not permitted to operate outside the declared purposes of the trust, however worthwhile or charitable those other purposes may be. This means, for example, that a trust whose Memorandum declared its object as "To preserve for the benefit of the townspeople of Weston in the County of Oldshire and of the nation at large, whatever of the historical, architectural and constructional heritage may exist in Weston aforesaid" would be unable to respond to a threat to a building in neighbouring Easton (whose townspeople, regrettably, had not thought fit to establish a trust).

Unless the intention is to form a county-wide trust, it is probably best to restrict the geographical range, so that the trust is genuinely local. There is much to be said for designating a distinct town, or a local planning authority area. The "beneficial area" might then be defined as "in Weston and surrounding districts", or "in and around the Borough of Weston", or "in and around the District of Weston".

The trust's name

The trust's name should relate to its objects and beneficial area, and indicate clearly what the trust is all about: in other words, the name should refer both to **preservation** and to the **locality** in which preservation will be undertaken. The obvious choices will therefore be "Weston and District Buildings Preservation Trust", "Weston Historic Buildings Trust", "Weston, Easton and District Preservation Trust Ltd", or variations on these. It is probably better for public relations, and especially for fund raising, if the name does not include the word "Limited". Permission to omit "Ltd" should be sought from the Registrar of Companies.

Membership of the trust

The Memorandum and Articles of Association will set out the rights and duties of **members of the trust,** who are broadly equivalent to shareholders in a company limited by shares. All trust members have the **right** to vote at meetings and a **liability** (limited to the amount stipulated in the Memorandum) to contribute to any debts at the time of the trust's dissolution.

A number of points should be borne in mind when deciding who will be the first members of the trust (those who sign the trust's Memorandum and Articles of Association), and how large its eventual membership should be.

Minimum number of members

Legally, a trust can have as few as two members: this is the minimum number required by the Companies Act 1985 to enjoy the benefits of limited liability. The Memorandum and Articles can therefore be signed by as few as two people, who will be known as the trust's "subscribers". Subscribers automatically become members of the trust.

An upper limit?

There need be no upper limit to membership of the trust, but it is quite normal for the Articles of Association to stipulate a maximum number.

Figure 12 — *British Historic Buildings Trust had plenty of space in which to advertise its transformation of Forge Row in Cwmavon, Gwent. The listed terrace of iron-workers' cottages had been derelict for 15 years. The AHF loaned £75,000 of the £270,000 working capital required.*

Large membership can have advantages: members can be charged a subscription, for example, and encouraged to support and promote the trust in various ways which a small group might find more difficult. But a large membership can give rise to certain practical problems:

> By law, all members must be notified at least 14 days in advance of each Annual General Meeting and any Extraordinary General Meeting that may be convened.

> A small voluntary organisation will find it onerous to "service" a large membership, eg

> — keeping mailing lists;
> — sending out notices;
> — hiring a room big enough to accommodate those entitled to attend meetings;
> — circulating a newsletter;
> — devising a programme to hold members' interest;
> — including the names and details of all members in the trust's annual return to the Registrar of Companies.

> It is often the members of the trust who elect members of the management committee (see below).

"Friends" of the trust

An alternative, which will keep formal membership within manageable limits but enable the trust to involve a wider public in some of its affairs, is to introduce the concept of "Friends" of the trust. Friends do not have the right to attend annual general meetings etc, but can be sent newsletters, invited to events — and encouraged to support the trust with donations or in other ways.

The management of the trust

The Articles of Association will also set out the terms of reference of the trust's **management committee.** For convenience, this committee will be referred to below as the **Council of Management;** other possibilities are the **Board** or **Committee of Management, Board of Directors,** or **Executive Committee.**

Whatever its name, the management committee is the equivalent, in company law, of a Board of Directors. Members of the committee are however additionally responsible for the general control and administration of the BPT as a charity, and are thus effectively charity trustees. (Members of the management committees of some BPTs are indeed called "Trustees", even though the BPT is a limited liability company.)

Size and composition of the Council of Management

The Articles of Association will stipulate not only the name of the management committee, but also its size and membership.

The Council of Management may not by law have fewer than three members. Members of the management committee do not have to be (but normally are) members of the trust. Conversely, it is possible for every member of the trust to be a member of the management committee, and for the trust to have no other members.

The upper limit will depend on the character of the trust: a county-wide revolving fund, established at local authority initiative, is likely to need a larger Council of Management than a local revolving fund established by a few private individuals, so that a sufficient number both of local government members and/or officials and of lay people can participate in the decision-making process.

Those responsible for forming a BPT may find it prudent (to avoid the tedium and expense of amending the Articles of Association at a later stage) to set an upper limit to membership of the Council of Management somewhat higher than the number of members actually envisaged.

The size of the management committee should be determined principally by practical, not public relations or "political" considerations. The most important of these is that decision-taking must be as efficient and streamlined as possible: trusts with large Councils of Managements are often slow to respond to threats to particular buildings, and generally take much longer than smaller trusts to get projects under way.

Responsibilities of the Council of Management

Members of the Council of Management have clear powers and responsibilities not only under company law, but also as charity trustees.

Under the Companies Act 1985, the "Directors" are responsible for the control of the company (in this case, the BPT) and the management of its business. They are required to appoint a Company Secretary, and to ensure that accounts are properly kept, professionally audited, and filed annually with the Registrar of Companies.

The Memorandum and Articles of Association also lay down duties comparable to those of Charity Trustees, namely to apply the trust's income solely to projects which will promote the object of the trust, and to protect its assets. Among their other general duties trustees, in this case the Council of Management, are required to ensure that any money not immediately required is invested in such a way that it will maximise the benefit to the trust. (There are a number of efficient ways for trusts to maximise their investment return, for example through the Charities Deposit Account.) They are also required to obtain the Charity Commission's consent before mortgaging or selling property owned by the trust. This is dealt with in greater detail in Chapter Six.

Charity Trustees, like Company Directors, are required to keep proper accounts. It is advisable for trusts to send their accounts annually to the Charity Commission, even though the present requirement is only for trusts to make them available on request.

Restrictions on members of the Council of Management

As charity trustees, members of the Council of Management must work for the trust on a purely voluntary basis. They can be reimbursed for reasonable out-of-pocket expenses, and may even be paid for certain professional services, provided this is allowed for in the trust's Memorandum of Association. But the Charity Commissioners are not able to agree to the remuneration of Council Members in general terms. This means that without specific authority from the Charity Commissioners, no management committee member can be appointed to a salaried office of the trust, or to any office of the trust paid by fees. The Charity Commissioners will however consider sympathetically any particular case made to them where it seems essential for a Council Member to be paid for professional services rendered, or for a key paid employee to serve as a Council member. In such cases, the Charity Commisioners will normally allow the inclusion of a clause in the governing instrument of the charity in question, conferring the power by reference to the Council member either by name or by office.

This should be remembered when electing or appointing to the management committee people on whom the trust might wish to call for professional advice. It may not be possible, for example, for the trust to commission an architect or surveyor member of the Council of Management to undertake its first (or any subsequent) project, or to instruct a solicitor member of the Council to do the trust's conveyancing, in return for a fee. It is probably best therefore to avoid the appointment to the Council of people who may be asked to be act for the trust professionally, and to instead to invite them to attend relevant meetings in an advisory capacity. See also some comments on this in Chapter Four.

Terms of office

The Articles of Association will stipulate the manner in which members of the Council of Management are appointed or elected, and their terms of office. It is common practice for terms to run for anything between two and five years. Whatever the duration, it will be necessary for the Articles of Association to provide for the rotation of members of the Council of Management. The Architectural Heritage Fund *Model* provides that one-third should retire from office each year.

Opinions differ about the merits of allowing members to be reappointed or re-elected immediately their terms expire, or insisting on an interval of at least one year. The first course offers the certain benefit of continuity; the second a mechanism for painlessly getting rid of a member or members whose contribution to the trust is unhelpful.

Officers and committees of the trust

The Articles of Association should also set out the procedure for electing someone to the Chair, and make provision for the Council of Management to delegate its powers to a committee or committees of members of the Council. It should be noted, however, that charity trustees have no power to delegate entire responsibility for the administration of their charity, and that all acts and proceedings of committees and officers must be reported as soon as possible to the full body of trustees (the Council of Management).

As with terms of office for members of the management committee, there are differing views about the desirability of requiring the Chair to stand down for an interval at the end of his/her term, rather than being eligible for immediate reappointment. This is something which those responsible for setting up a trust must settle for themselves, after considered discussion.

CHAPTER FOUR

SETTING UP A REVOLVING FUND TRUST

This chapter describes the practical steps to be taken by anyone thinking of establishing a buildings preservation trust. It should be read in conjunction with Chapter Three, which explains the legal framework, terminology and formalities.

Making a start

Inspired, perhaps, by a threat to a particular building, a group of people decide to form a preservation trust. The initiative may be taken by two or three enthusiasts, by an existing organisation such as an amenity society or residents' association, or by a local authority.

Whatever its origins, a revolving fund trust will need to be able to command the interest and loyal support of a representative cross section of the community. On no account however must it be weighed down by cumbersome committee structures that delay decision-making, nor distracted from doing preservation projects by the need to keep a large membership informed and involved.

A steering committee

To take matters forward, those principally responsible for the initiative to form a trust should set up a small steering committee or working party to consider the proposed trust's aims and area of operation and to decide in the light of this what type of trust would be appropriate.

Figure 13 — *The Historic, Environmental and Architectural Rehabilitation Trust borrowed £5,000 from the AHF in 1982 to rehabilitate this 18th century lock-keeper's cottage in Drumbeg, Co Down.*

The steering committee would benefit from the advice of, and might therefore include or involve:

— a representative of the local civic or amenity society;
— someone with recent or current experience of a local authority planning department (eg a retired County Architect, Conservation Officer or County Planning Officer);
— an architect with a track record for projects which involve conservation work;
— a solicitor with experience of company law and charities;
— a chartered accountant;
— a bank manager;
— someone from an established and successful BPT in the same or a nearby county, and/or someone with personal experience of renovating an old building.

Above all, members of the steering committee, and — even more so — of the trust once established, should be enthusiastic and able as well as willing to carry responsibility and to get things done.

The local authority

Whether or not the steering committee includes a local authority representative (serving in a voluntary capacity), members should talk to the local authority about their plans at an early stage, since the interest, co-operation and — preferably — support of Councillors and officials can make all the difference to the ease with which the trust will be able to operate. This is because local authorities have responsibility in a number of areas which affect anyone planning to rehabilitate a building, namely:

Almost all building work, and all work which involves any change in the use of a building, requires **planning permission** from the local authority planning department.

Almost all work to a listed building requires **listed building consent** over and above planning permission.

Building work has to be approved, in advance and periodically as work proceeds, by the local authority's **building inspector.**

Local authorities administer **grant** for the repair and renovation of dwellings and the conversion of buildings into dwellings (see Chapter Eight).

Local authorities administer **grant** for the repair or maintenance of historic buildings (see Chapter Eight).

Local authorities should be able to help and advise trusts generally about buildings at risk and/or available for preservation in their area. In particular, local authorities are empowered to serve **repairs notices** on owners of historic buildings, and to initiate **compulsory purchase** proceedings if the owner fails to carry out works specified in the repairs notice within a period of two months. Local authorities may well wish to pass on buildings acquired by compulsory purchase to preservation trusts.

Getting to grips with the formalities

Deciding on "objects", area and name

The steering committee's first specific task will be to decide on the **"objects"**, **"beneficial area"** and **name** of the trust they propose to form (see Chapter Three). Although the name should indicate what the trust is all about, it should not be too cumbersome or lengthy — unless there is an obvious acronym.

Choosing the first members

Next, the steering committee will need to decide who will sign the trust's Memorandum and Articles and how large its membership should be. They should remember that those who sign automatically become members of the trust.

Setting up the management committee

Having settled these questions, the steering committee should discuss the trust's **management committee** (the "Council of Management"). They will need to decide how large it should be; whether members should be elected or appointed, and by whom; and what officers the committee should elect and appoint.

In addition to the various legal requirements described in Chapter Three, the steering committee should bear in mind a number of other points when considering the size and composition of the management committee.

The efficient conduct of business

Building preservation projects cannot be managed by committees. Even though the trust's aim is altruistic and its object charitable, every project it undertakes is, and must be approached as, a commercial operation. Large sums of money will be at stake, and market forces mean that there will always be an element of risk. The trust will be entering into contractual commitments, dealing professionally with architects, surveyors, bankers, builders, officials, estate agents and lawyers. Decisions will often need to be taken quickly; bills must be paid promptly. It must therefore have an effective management structure.

The position of "professionals"

A trust can derive great benefit from the advice of relevant professionals — architects and surveyors, for example. But there are disadvantages to having such people on the Council of Management:

> There is always a danger that an architect intimately associated with a trust will obtain the lion's share of its work, even though another local architect might be the best for the project or the lowest on fees.

> An architect associated with a trust may be tempted to suggest projects in the hope that he or his partnership will receive the commission. Real problem buildings may thus be inadvertently overlooked in favour of good "architects'" projects.

> Members of the Council of Management must be able to meet without the professional concerned

being present. They will need, for example, to discuss in confidence an architect's fee, performance, and suitability for a project.

It may be prudent, therefore, to include as members of the Council of Management only people who are not in a position to provide professional services to the trust (or who have made it clear that they will not do work for the trust in return for a fee), and to invite appropriate professionals to act as honorary advisers, if they are willing to do so.

The trust's officers

The steering committee will need to give some thought to the trust's first office holders: essentially, someone to take the **Chair,** and someone to fill the post — required by law — of **Company Secretary.** The Company Secretary must be appointed by the "directors" (members of the Council of Management). He/she can be a member of the Council of Management, provided the post carries no salary or fee. Equally the Company Secretary can be a member of the trust's staff (if it has any staff), or someone from outside the organisation, paid or unpaid.

Many trusts elect or appoint a Treasurer. There is no need to designate other posts, but among those designated by some trusts are the offices of a project manager, meetings secretary, events secretary, fund-raising secretary, etc.

Horses for courses

Unless the trust is large enough to permit and warrant the delegation of day to day executive authority to a committee, or the appointment of one or more paid members of staff, office holders must be people qualified and willing to roll up their sleeves on the trust's behalf. Letterhead figures (local dignitaries etc) may impress potential donors, but if the person elected or appointed to the Chair has been chosen principally for this purpose, he or she must be supported by a Secretary or Treasurer who is authorised to get on with the real work of the trust.[1]

Finance and registration

Money

It is not essential at this stage to think about big money, the start-up capital for a project, but there will be an early requirement for modest sums (not exceeding £750), in order to pay the fees involved in establishing and incorporating the trust as a legal entity, print its letterhead (something on which it is probably not worth cutting corners for the sake of economy), etc.

Although the immediate requirement is relatively small, the steering committee ought also to draw up an outline financial strategy. It should also consider registering the trust for VAT (see Chapter Seven).

---

[1]But see Chapter Three on delegation to committees/staff and the responsibility of "trustees".

The subject of fund-raising is dealt with in Chapter Eight. At this stage, even though times are hard, it may be worth approaching the local authority for a start-up grant, particularly if the trust has already targeted a building as its first project. The steering committee could also approach prominent local businesses etc for seed-corn capital for the trust, or try to persuade a parent organisation (if there is one — eg the local civic society), or another sympathetic body, to agree to pay bills which come in before the trust is formally established — particularly before it is in a position to open a bank account in its own name.

Legal advice and incorporation

As soon as the steering committee has agreed in principle to establish a trust, has decided its aims, beneficial area, and size, and has sufficient money to pay for the formalities, it should instruct a solicitor — preferably one who is familiar with both company and charity law — or a company agent to draw up the trust's Memorandum and Articles of Association and undertake its incorporation by registering the trust with the Registrar of Companies.

Provided the steering committee does not depart from the AHF *Model* (see Chapter Three and Appendix D), this should be straightforward, not unduly costly and relatively quick — but registration, particularly with the Charity Commission, can take months rather than weeks. This should be allowed for when planning a first project, not least because the Architectural Heritage Fund is required by law to restrict its low-interest loans to organisations with charitable status, and will need to see a copy of the letter to the trust from the Charity Commission or — in Scotland and Northern Ireland — from the Inland Revenue confirming this status.

Obtaining charitable status

It is advisable for people forming a trust in England and Wales, or the solicitor acting for them, to consult the Charity Commission at the earliest possible stage, forwarding a copy of the proposed Memorandum and Articles of Association *in draft*. Addresses of Charity Commission offices will be found in Appendix G.

When making a formal request for charitable status, the following documents will be required:

> One certified and one other copy of the organisation's incorporated Memorandum and Articles. If the AHF *Model* has been used, this should be stated and any amendments pointed out.

> Full information about how the organisation proposes to achieve its aims.

> Copies of minutes of meetings, newspaper cuttings, appeal literature, etc, which may serve to illustrate the work of the organisation.

Ready to go!

As soon as the trust has been incorporated, it can get down to the work to which all the foregoing is merely preliminary!

Figure 14 — *No. 3 Quay Walls, Berwick-upon-Tweed, Northumberland, occupies a prime position facing the Tweed. Built as a granary in the late 18th century, it was unloved and neglected during most of the post-war period.*

Figure 15 — *Berwick-upon-Tweed Preservation Trust acquired 3 Quay Walls in 1983. The AHF loaned £150,000 towards the cost of restoring and converting the building into residential, office and workshop accommodation.*

Figure 16 — *As its sixth project, Teesdale BPT took on a small disused stable block in King Street, Barnard Castle, Co Durham (see also figs. 8 and 9).*

Figure 17 — *The Trust borrowed £45,000 from the AHF in 1987 to convert 17 King Street into two houses for sale.*

Figure 18 — *Romsey & District BPT came to the aid of this thatched cottage in distress in Whitenap Lane, Romsey, Hampshire, in 1987.*

Figure 19 — *The AHF loaned £25,000 to help the Trust put things right.*

CHAPTER FIVE

GEARING UP FOR A PROJECT

This chapter assumes that the trust has completed the formalities described in Chapters Three and Four, and that a Council of Management capable of carrying out the trust's business with professional confidence and competence is in place. This may require a decision by the Council to delegate responsibility for all aspects of the management of a project to not more than two Council members, so that work is not held up while meetings are convened to authorise action on this or that. The people concerned must, however, report regularly to the Council of Management.

Getting all the pieces in place for a project is a complex and time-consuming process. A new trust should not be discouraged if its first — or second, or third — attempt founders. Trusts which claim to be unable to find a building at risk should instead take the first appropriate opportunity to carry out **an exemplary scheme** to counter the progressively damaging incidence of insensitive alterations to historic buildings, which is as serious a threat to the nation's heritage as dereliction.

Finding a property

Some trusts are formed in response to a threat to a particular building. This section is addressed to those which need to find a property to tackle.

There is no single, or simple, formula for finding a building that both needs and merits preservation, **and** is available, **and** whose acquisition the trust can finance. Established trusts report widely differing experience, some having to turn suitable buildings away because they are already up to their eyes in a project or projects, others unable over extended periods to find any building at all. Given the numbers of buildings at risk throughout the country, a trust with sufficient determination, backed up by an effective decision-making structure, should always be able to locate and get hold of a building to preserve and rehabilitate.

The local authority

If no building immediately presents itself, a newly-formed trust should talk to the local authority planning department, and to the Conservation Officer if there is one. The trust might offer to take a redundant (but preferably not too complex) building off the authority's hands, perhaps following a repairs notice and compulsory purchase order, and should certainly seek the help of the planning department in locating a building suitable for BPT treatment.

"Buildings at Risk" and "Over the Shop"

A second source for ideas is English Heritage, in particular its "Buildings at Risk" section. A third is the University of York's "Over the Shop" project. (See Appendix C for further information, including addresses and telephone numbers.) As part of the search, but also as a useful exercise in itself, the trust could do its own survey of buildings at risk in the area, first consulting the local authority in case it has already initiated such a survey and/or would like the trust to follow the pro forma devised by English Heritage.

Preliminaries to purchase

As soon as the trust has identified a potential project, it should obtain a preliminary estimate of the costs involved (including the purchase price) and of the property's eventual resale value.

The importance of feasibility studies

Unless a trust member or adviser is qualified and willing to do a back-of-the-envelope feasibility study and estimate free of charge, the trust will need at this stage to commission an architect or surveyor with experience of conservation work to inspect the building, note obvious structural and other problems, recommend both essential and optional alterations and put a figure to the likely cost of the work to be done. If the project is complicated and expensive, for example involving a major element of conversion from one use to another and elaborate repairs, the trust should commission a full feasibility study — not necessarily from the architect it intends to use for the project itself.

"End use" and resale value

At this stage too an estate agent or chartered surveyor should be asked to recommend the most appropriate eventual use for the building in the light of local market conditions, and to estimate its likely selling price after restoration and/or conversion. It is important to choose a firm or individual with specialist knowledge of the market to provide this advice and estimate, particularly if the project will include conversion.

Planning permission

If the project is likely to involve a change in the use of the building, the trust will need to ascertain how easy or difficult it will be to obtain planning permission for the change, and listed building consent for the alterations, before deciding to proceed.

Vacant possession

The trust should satisfy itself as far as possible (short of instructing a lawyer to investigate title) as to the building's availability, freehold or leasehold with vacant possession. It should also take whatever steps may be necessary or appropriate to persuade the owner to part with it, preferably for less than its market value or with payment of the full purchase price deferred until the trust is ready to put the building back on the market after rehabilitation.

Sources of concessionary finance

Armed with rough estimates, the next step is for the trust to approach English Heritage (or its equivalent in Scotland, Wales and Northern Ireland), the local authority, the Architectural Heritage Fund and other relevant organisations to ascertain what may be forthcoming by way of grant, interest-free or low-interest loans (see Chapter Eight). If the prospects look reasonable, the trust should obtain application forms and start pencilling in the information required, so that formal applications can be despatched as soon as the project is ready to go ahead.

Information about sources of "official" finance is included in Chapter Eight, but trusts are urged to take nothing at face value and to check the current position with each organisation before assuming that Chapter Eight is up to date, as requirements and conditions governing grants frequently change. **It will be important to the trust's cash flow also to ascertain the timetable to which each grant or loan-making organisation works, and as far as possible to schedule the project so that there is the minimum gap between payments due to the vendor, contractor, architect, etc, and an inflow of concessionary finance.**

Putting in a bid

The trust is now ready to take the plunge and make a conditional offer — subject if possible not only to contract but also to obtaining planning permission and listed building consent — based on its own and an estate agent's view of what the building is worth. In Scotland, an offer is a binding commitment: negotiations over price etc will have to take place before the offer is made, and the trust will have to instruct a solicitor to act for it at this stage.

In England and Wales, negotiations can take place after the offer is made. The trust should think very carefully before increasing its offer if the owner does not at first accept: this is the trust's first project, and it has neither the experience nor, probably, the capital to justify competing with a private sector buyer (as a more experienced trust might do) on the grounds that the trust will do a better job in repairing the building than another restoring purchaser. Except in parts of the south and south east of England, it is in fact unlikely that anyone else will put in a serious bid for a property of the kind envisaged.

If the building is listed and in a poor state of preservation, and the owner is reluctant to part with it, the trust could try to persuade the local authority to initiate the repairs notice/compulsory purchase order procedure, by undertaking to buy the building from the local authority when the procedure has run its course.

Formalising the project

As soon as the offer has been accepted, the trust should instruct a solicitor to act for it on the purchase and, provided searches etc are going smoothly and completion looks certain, appoint a chartered surveyor or architect to survey the building. Before embarking on the many tasks described in Chapter Six, the trust should now prepare a budget and draw up a cash flow statement. Details will need to be filled in or amended as tenders etc are submitted, but it should be possible even at this stage to assess whether or not it will be necessary to arrange an overdraft facility with a bank or building society and launch a fund-raising campaign.

Figure 20 — *Leegomery Mill, near Telford in Shropshire, ground flour until 1945. In 1978 it was badly damaged by fire.*

Figure 21 — *Shropshire BPT borrowed £32,500 from the AHF in 1988 to restore and convert Leegomery Mill into a house.*

The project budget

It is essential both to budget and to plan the flow of cash efficiently.

Expenditure will include not only the obvious major items like purchase, building works and the project architect's fee, but a range of other items, for example:

- payment for specialist services (a feasibility study; reports by quantity surveyors, structural engineers, etc);
- legal fees (arising not only from the purchase and sale of the property, but also from the negotiation of any charges — mortgages — that have to be given as security for loans);
- planning application charges (listed building consents are free);
- the building inspector;
- insurance, both of the building and against liability for accidents etc affecting personnel;
- interest payments (to the bank or building society, the Architectural Heritage Fund, and any other lenders);
- VAT (see below, and Chapter Seven);
- the estate agent's commission;
- landscaping and planting;
- fixtures and fittings;
- miscellaneous and contingency.

Income will consist of grants, loans, interest on capital (if any!), proceeds of general fund-raising (if undertaken), and the eventual resale of the property.

Contingency planning

Trusts should always have a contingency plan in case a grant is not paid. The finances should look on a percentage of grant aid as a bonus. As a rule of thumb, a trust should also assume the worst of VAT, ie that it will be liable for full VAT and no recovery, though it should make every effort to recover the maximum possible (see also Chapter Seven). Failure to do so, or to allow for this in the budget, can — in the words of one trust — make the difference between delight and disaster.

The cash flow statement

Once the budget is ready, the trust should draw up a cash flow statement, setting out income and expenditure on a month by month basis so that it is possible to see at once the extent and timing of the trust's borrowing and other cash requirements (see sample cash flow statement in Appendix A).

Security for loans

If the trust expects to have to borrow from a bank or building society, and intends to apply to the Architectural Heritage Fund for a low-interest loan, it will need to offer security for the amount borrowed. Security can take time to negotiate, and this should be allowed for when planning the cash flow statement and programme of work.

The AHF, for example, requires **either** a first charge on the building (if — as in the case of the prototype in Appendix A — it is to be sold after rehabilitation), **or** a formal guarantee of repayment from a bank, local authority or comparable corporate body. Negotiating a first charge involves lawyers, who — even though the trust's solicitor will have gone over the same ground — may uncover unexpected problems with title.

Negotiating a repayment guarantee can require the trust to provide the guarantor with back-to-back security. This may take the form of a mortgage on the building, which will be susceptible to the same delays as when the AHF takes a first charge.

The trust should bear in mind that if either the AHF or a repayment guarantor has a first charge on the building, it will need to persuade other lenders to take a second charge, or to accept some other form of security. In some cases trust members individually provide security for a loan or guarantee from a bank. While this demonstrates a laudable degree of commitment to the project, anyone contemplating such a step should understand that lenders will not necessarily agree to an extension if the trust cannot repay a loan on schedule. In such a case the repayment guarantor would be called upon to repay the loan — and would in turn be likely to call upon those who provided security for the guarantee.

Charity Commission permission to borrow

Under Section 29 of the Charities Act 1960, a trust incorporated in England or Wales will need the formal consent of the Charity Commission to any proposal to mortgage or charge property which is held by the trust and is or has at any time been occupied for the purposes of the trust as security for a loan. When a trust purchases a building with the intention of ensuring its preservation (in accordance with its charitable object), then it is deemed that the property is functionally occupied as soon as the trust and/or its agents enter on to the property with this end in view. In granting consent, the Charity Commission will normally wish to be satisfied that the mortgaging is in the best interests of the charity.

Obtaining the Charity Commission's consent to a mortgage can take time. This should be allowed for when planning the programme of work and the cash flow, since the Architectural Heritage Fund, for example, cannot contract a loan secured by a first charge on the building until it has evidence of Charity Commission consent to the transaction.

Purchase!

Assuming that neither the lawyer, architect or surveyor, the trust's treasurer or anyone else finds any reason to think again about the proposed project, and the money is available to do so, the trust can now complete its purchase of the building.

Figure 22 — *Grade II* listed, timber-framed, 18th century buildings in Gravesend High Street, Kent, before their reprieve from ruin by Kent BPT (see also fig 43 p. 72).*

CHAPTER SIX

MANAGING THE PROJECT

From the moment the trust formally decides to purchase the property, until the time comes to put the restored building on the market, its role will be to manage, co-ordinate and pay those responsible for executing work undertaken on the trust's behalf. As proprietor and client, the trust — through the member or members authorised to manage the project (referred to from now on as "the project manager") — is in charge of a major commercial operation. The effort involved should not be under-estimated — but nor should the rewards.

A photographic record

It may seem odd to begin this chapter with a section on something as apparently marginal as photography. Keeping a photographic record is however no optional extra, but an essential part of the process — and it should start before the first barrow-load of rubbish is removed, scaffold erected or contractor's board put up. The photographs need not be up to professional standard, but must be sufficiently competent to illustrate the condition of the property when the trust took it over, and the changes which take place as work proceeds — to both the exterior and the interior of the building.

There are several reasons why a photographic record is necessary as well as desirable. The trust will almost certainly need to supply photographs when applying for grants and loans, for example. Depending on the nature of the project, it may need to show photographs to the VAT inspector, in order to demonstrate the extent to which the work involved "substantial reconstruction" (see Chapter Seven). Photographs of the building before restoration will also be invaluable for publicity — both for fund-raising, and when the time comes to put the property on the market.

A site notice-board

For publicity purposes, the project manager should also arrange to erect a notice-board at the site, proclaiming that the building has been acquired for restoration by the trust. This will be joined in due course by a board erected by the contractor, which should be large enough to contain space for notices advertising the contribution to the project of English Heritage, the Architectural Heritage Fund and others.

Insurance

Probably the first formal move the project manager should make once the building is trust property is to take out insurance cover, not only against damage etc to the building itself, but also — if the trust has not

Figure 23 — *The Old Castle Land Trust needed local support as well as a £23,000 loan from the AHF to restore this unusual property in Bishop's Castle, Shropshire, in 1988. Built in the 15th or 16th centuries, the House on Crutches is listed Grade II* and is an Ancient Monument.*

Figure 24 — *Scruffy shop fronts conceal a 16th century property with two super-imposed medieval halls and the largest medieval moulded timber window to have survived in Norwich. Norwich Preservation Trust is giving the buildings a new lease of life as an art gallery and recital room, with flats above.*

already done this for other reasons — public and employers' liability for any accidents etc which may occur on site. The contractor, once appointed, is bound to have liability insurance, but the trust will be liable both before and after the period of the contract.

Appointing professionals

Choosing the right architect

The second formal move is to appoint the architect for the project. In some areas, there may be virtually no choice, unless the trust is prepared to look relatively far afield. Wherever possible, however, the architect should be selected because he or his firm is right for this particular job, not because he is known personally to a member or members of the trust or has the biggest practice in the town.

The right architect for a BPT project will be one who has specialist experience as well as the basic competence indicated by a professional qualification. It is just as mistaken to think that more or less any architect will have the skills needed for a preservation project as it would be to think that any doctor could perform an intricate surgical operation. Some architects may be competent to carry out ordinary refurbishment, but not when this has to be combined with historic preservation. Others will be renowned for restoring brick buildings, but with no expertise in stone or timber. Some will be too busy; others will have spare capacity. The project manager should interview several architects, asking about their work, interests, fee basis, and approach to this particular project. He should also ask for references, and for examples of work undertaken.

The Royal Institution of British Architects (RIBA) has recently introduced a new fee basis, one for "normal" refurbishment/conversion, the other for work on specified historic buildings. But architects are also used to "fee bidding", ie offering their services at below RIBA rates. This is quite acceptable amongst reputable architects in the profession and causes no embarrassment. A trust would do well to obtain Fee Bids from three architects before making an appointment — but should be aware that the cheapest may well not be the best for the particular job.

Preparing a brief

The trust will need to give the architect, once appointed, a brief to which to work. This may be prepared by the trust alone, or in consultation with the architect. If the former, the architect should probably be given an opportunity to comment before the brief is put into final form, since it will constitute the trust's formal instructions, and the scope for later misunderstandings will be greatly reduced if the architect has himself made an input.

This brief cannot be written until fundamental decisions have been taken by the trust, again perhaps in consultation with the architect and certainly in the light of local market conditions, about the eventual use of the building. If there is to be any element of conversion — into flats, offices, shops below/offices or flats above, etc — grant-giving bodies, and the local planning authority, may wish to express a view.

Once agreed, the brief will serve as the framework for the project, to be filled in by the architect's instructions to the contractor, which in turn will be further amplified by the detailed **specification** from the contractor. The brief should therefore summarise the main features of the project — the character and present condition of the building, the end-use envisaged, the principal structural work required, the period features which must be preserved, the extent to which the interior will need to be altered, the trust's wishes in respect of the types of materials to be used. Either in the brief itself, or elsewhere, the trust should refer to the fee basis on which the architect is to be engaged, and stipulate that the architect may not issue instructions which raise the

cost of the project without the project manager's prior approval.

Choosing a contractor

The architect's first task (assuming the property was thoroughly surveyed prior to purchase — see Chapter Five) will be to produce drawings — both plans and elevations — of the building as existing and as proposed. Wherever possible, the architect should work in consultation with the local planning authority's conservation officer to ensure that he/she is happy with the alterations envisaged, materials to be used, etc. (Regrettably, all too many local authorities do not have a conservation officer.) When the trust has approved the drawings, the architect should invite tenders for the work to be done. The invitation will broadly follow the brief for the project and contain specific instructions about the materials to be used, historic features to be preserved, etc.

The tendering process can cause anxiety, particularly if price quotations come in disagreeably higher than anticipated and require the budget and cash flow statement to be radically revised. The project manager and the architect should evaluate bids together, bearing in mind that the lowest tender will not necessarily be the best and that there will be good reasons for dramatic variations in price quotations. The architect should bring to the discussion first-hand, or at least reliable second-hand, opinion of comparable work done by each contractor elsewhere, and seek references on their reliability and financial standing.

Permissions and finance

Planning permission and listed building consent

In parallel with going out to tender, the architect will be preparing formal applications to the local authority for planning permission and listed building consent. (There is a fee for planning permission, but none for listed building consent.) At the same time, the project manager should start to complete applications for every grant and/or loan for which the project may be eligible, so that these can be despatched at the earliest opportunity (see Chapters Five and Eight).

Local authority planning departments will ask to see detailed specifications and costings before granting planning permission and listed building consent. Both local authority and other grant and loan-making organisations will also need to see specifications and costings before releasing, and in some cases before approving, funds.

English Heritage grant

The project manager should get to know his local English Heritage Section 10 and Section 3A architects, so that plans for the building can be discussed informally before the trust submits a formal grant application.

When the costs rise . . .

If detailed costings amount to more than the trust had estimated and can afford, the project manager should be careful to ensure that only those items which are of marginal importance to the long-term preservation of the building are dispensed with or cut back. The trust should not, for example, opt for cheaper, non-traditional roof tiles or for brand-name windows; nor can it skimp on fundamentals like damp and wood-worm treatment, repointing, and quality rainwater goods. The trust's reputation, and indeed the charitable object of the operation, will be at risk if corners are cut. Moreover grant-making organisations may well reduce or even withhold finance if the work proposed falls short of the standard expected of a preservation project.

Rather than trim the project back and look for corners to cut if every tender is too high, the trust should step up its fund-raising efforts. It should also be sure to include every known or potential expense when applying for grants, since the amounts offered will often be based on gross estimates of cost.

Once work starts

Keeping abreast

Once the trust has appointed a contractor, adjusted the cash flow statement to include all scheduled expenditure, loan and grant income, and obtained the necessary planning permissions and/or listed building consent, it should agree with the architect a date for work to begin on site. Detailed supervision of the work, and dealings with the building inspector and contractor, should be undertaken by the architect, who will also be responsible for certifying the contractor's invoices and asking the trust for payment as work proceeds. **But the trust can never assume that things are happening as and when they should. No matter how meticulous and active the architect, the project manager must keep abreast of every aspect of the project at every stage, particularly finance and financial contracts. He must check and double check that**

nothing is left undone by those who should be responsible, and be on the spot to sort out each problem as soon as it arises.

There is a fine line to be drawn between *management* and *interference*. The project manager should know exactly what is being done, by whom, and when. He should attend regular meetings between the architect and contractor, and look in on the site at frequent, and irregular, intervals. Decisions may be needed in a hurry, particularly if demolition or clearance reveals unsuspected problems — or features of particular note, which may need to be studied by experts and perhaps recorded by archaeologists before being sealed over. But no matter how detailed his involvement with the work, the project manager should never give instructions to the contractor without the architect's prior knowledge and approval. And it is vital that even the smallest alteration of the specification is agreed by the relevant parties in writing before any action is taken.

Dealing with money

The project manager should ensure that he is in a position to respond promptly to requests for payment, for example by mustering the necessary signatures on cheques, drawing down loan instalments from the Architectural Heritage Fund, grant from English Heritage, etc. An architect's certificate — which confirms the validity of the contractor's invoice — is legally binding on the client and cannot be contested. To minimise the possibility of delays in making due payments, the project manager may wish to instruct the architect to send copies of certificates direct to the Architectural Heritage Fund and English Heritage, so that these funding organisations can despatch instalments in time for the trust to pay the contractor's bill.

Finishing touches

Well before the main building work nears an end, the project manager (and architect) should take decisions about fixtures and fittings, and about landscaping.

Figure 25 — *Even urban terraces should be enhanced by landscaping — in progress here at Railway Cottages, Derby (see also p. 13 and figs. 11, 30 and 31).*

Fixtures and fittings

If the building is intended for residential use, the trust will need to install basic kitchen and bathroom fittings. The project manager would be wise to go for the plainest (but not necessarily the cheapest) of the range. When in doubt, stick to simple white — both in the bathroom and in the kitchen. A purchaser who wants an avocado bathroom suite with gold-plated taps, or beige kitchen cupboards with dark brown trim and fancy door knobs, is likely also to want a particular make or style, and will not hesitate to throw out whatever the trust has installed. Anyone else will be happy to live with something plain and inoffensive, at least for a few months.

Landscaping

However large or small the area of land surrounding the property may be, the project manager should ensure that it is at least cleared of contractors' rubble, and preferably landscaped, before putting the property on the market. The trust owes the building an attractive immediate environment. It will also enhance sales prospects if prospective purchasers do not have to tramp through weeds and mud, but can approach the building along a path through an embryonic garden planted with a few young shrubs.

Garages

Estate agents often put pressure on trusts to equip houses with garages. Such pressure should in general be resisted, as a garage will seldom increase the sale price to a point where the trust will recoup the additional expenditure incurred in its construction. Instead, the trust should supply architect's drawings, a specification of the materials and location, and pass these — together with the necessary planning permission — to the new owner.

Preparing to sell

Insurance

As soon as the contractor's work is finished, front-line responsibility for the building reverts to the trust. The project manager will need to attend to insurance — and to security, now that the property presents an attractive face to the world, including potential squatters and vandals.

Charity Commission consent

At this stage, if the building is in England or Wales, the project manager will need to pave the way for the sale by getting in touch with the Charity Commission. Under Section 29 of the Charities Act, trusts must seek the Charity Commission's consent to the proposed sale of a restored building and, before completing a sale, to satisfy the Charity Commissioners that the sale price is the best that can reasonably be obtained. A leaflet entitled "Selling Charity Land", available free of charge from the Charity Commission, explains this in greater detail.

The Charity Commission is likely also to require evidence that the trust has taken adequate steps to ensure the long-term preservation of the building, for example by imposing positive and restrictive preservation covenants (see below). Failure to do this could jeopardise the trust's charitable status.

Protecting the building against future alteration

Having taken so much trouble to restore the building, the trust will naturally wish to do everything possible to ensure that it cannot be aesthetically vandalised by a subsequent owner. This is a complex matter, in which English law and practice is less developed than Scottish. BPTs should therefore take legal advice at an early stage.

If the building is listed, its principal external features (and any internal features specifically mentioned in the listing Citation) will enjoy a measure of statutory protection, in that anyone who wishes to carry out alterations must first obtain listed building consent. But the trust may want to impose additional obligations upon future owners. It may consider, for example, that external alterations should require the prior approval of the trust, as well as listed building consent. In addition, the trust may want to protect other features from alteration, and to ensure that the property as a whole is kept in good repair. Unfortunately these fairly simple requirements can be rather difficult to achieve in practice because of complexities in the law relating to real property. The following comments about imposing **covenants** to ensure the building's long-term preservation apply only to England and Wales; Scottish trusts should take legal advice locally, as the law in Scotland is different.

Figure 26 — *Castle Park Arts Centre devoted almost as much attention to the garden as to preserving and converting the former stable block known as Clock Tower Building in Castle Park, Frodsham, Cheshire.*

Retaining the freehold

The most effective way of ensuring that both positive and restrictive covenants can be enforced against a future owner of the property is for the property to be sold by way of a long lease, which would normally be for a term of anything from 99 years upwards. The trust would retain the freehold and would find itself in a direct landlord/tenant relationship with the leasehold owner. This method has disadvantages, mainly the management required of the trust as the number of retained freeholds proliferates, but also the reduced attractiveness and marketability of a leasehold property as opposed to a freehold.

Imposing covenants

If the trust sells the freehold, then restrictive covenants can be imposed upon the first purchaser. These will be enforceable against future owners as long as the trust retains some property in the vicinity which is capable of benefiting from the covenants. The major problem, however, is that this method only permits enforceability of **restrictive** (as opposed to positive) covenants, and that it may not prove practicable for the trust to retain any neighbouring property. If the trust does not keep a toe-hold in or alongside the building, it will not be possible to enforce the restrictive covenants against the second or subsequent purchasers.

Another method, which one trust has found entirely satisfactory, is to require each successive purchaser to enter into a new Deed of Covenant (which can incorporate both positive and restrictive provisions) directly in favour of the trust. An example of such a Deed of Covenant is reproduced in Appendix E. On the occasion of the first sale by the trust, the Land Registry is instructed not to register any future owner as the proprietor of the property unless an appropriate Deed of Covenant has been entered into. This method is only foolproof where the title to the land is registered. In the case of unregistered land, the machinery does not exist for preventing the legal title passing until the Deed of Covenant has been given.

Marketing the building

When should the trust put the property on the market? Opinions differ, but whether or not it is formally advertised by an estate agent before rehabilitation is complete, the trust should do whatever it can to rouse local interest in the project, including the fact that the building will eventually be up for sale.

At whatever point the trust decides to market the property, the project manager should instruct the estate agent to advertise it not just as a desirable period house (or suite of offices, etc) for sale or lease, but as a historic building which has been rescued and rehabilitated by the local preservation trust. This ought both to add to the property's market appeal, and to promote knowledge of and interest in the trust.

Sale formalities

As soon as an offer has been accepted, the trust's solicitor should be instructed to negotiate with the prospective purchaser's solicitor, and to use as much as necessary of the sale proceeds to repay the Architectural Heritage Fund and any other lender who has a charge on the building.

An opening ceremony

Simultaneously with advertising the property and negotiating its sale, the trust should arrange some sort of ceremony to celebrate the completion of the project and attract publicity. It may wish to invite its Patron, if it has one, or a local dignitary, such as the mayor, to perform an "opening" (particularly if the local authority was involved with the project); alternatively someone from English Heritage, if it has provided grant, or the Architectural Heritage Fund, if it has provided loan finance, could be asked to officiate.

It is worth spending a bit of trust money on this ceremony, which should be a formal, but not lavish, public event. Members of the local authority should be invited; the local press should be present in force; and invitations should also be sent to anyone else whose interest might be beneficial in the short or longer term, or who has contributed to the project or helped the trust. There should be an opportunity for everyone to see over and round the building, in which the trust should mount a modest exhibition — photographs of the property in its unrestored condition, information about the trust itself, information about the project, acknowledgements to those who provided money and help. Simple refreshments should be offered. The official opening may take the form of the unveiling of a plaque, cutting of a ribbon, or just a few short speeches. If possible, these should include an announcement by the trust of its next project, and an appeal for help in raising the necessary finance . . . .

Figure 27 — *Opening ceremonies must proceed irrespective of the elements. Lord Montagu of Beaulieu doing the honours for North West BPT at Cockton's Yard in Cockermouth, Cumbria, in March 1987.*

CHAPTER SEVEN

VALUE ADDED TAX

VAT is a wide-ranging tax at a standard rate of 15% on most supplies of goods and services in the domestic economy, with certain reliefs being provided by means of "zero-rating" and "exemption". It is not proposed here to try to give more than a brief summary of the way in which this complex tax affects the work of BPTs, together with some suggestions for getting more detailed information and advice.

Charities not exempt

There is a common misconception that charities are somehow exempt from VAT or at least entitled to special treatment. In fact, although charitable status carries entitlement to certain fiscal reliefs from direct taxation (such as income tax and corporation tax), charities have usually paid consumer taxes and so there is no general relief for them in VAT legislation purely on account of their charitable status. The formation stage of a new trust is therefore the appropriate time for its Treasurer-designate to contact the local VAT officer (whose address will be found in the telephone directory) and obtain some of HM Customs & Excise's helpful explanatory leaflets.[1] If it is felt desirable to consult an accountant as well, be sure to choose one used to dealing with the complexities of VAT, and ideally one who has working knowledge of its application to the construction industry.

Relief through "zero-rating": dwellings and certain other buildings

In the preliminary costing out of any rehabilitation project, it is essential to take account of any VAT which you will be charged, not only on the building work and materials but on all professional services involved (architect, quantity surveyor, solicitor, estate agent, etc). However, limited or full relief from VAT may be available if all or part of the goods and services you buy in for a project are zero-rated (ie made technically taxable at a nil rate).

---

[1]Value Added Tax: General Guide (Notice 700)

Should I be registered for VAT? (700/1/88)

The Ins and Outs of VAT (700/15A/87)

VAT: Keeping Records and Accounts (700/21/87)

Filling in your VAT Return (700/12/87)

VAT: Partial Exemption (Notice 706)

VAT: Protected buildings (708/1/85) and Amendment 2, which reflects liability changes contained in the 1989 Finance Bill.

VAT: Construction Industry (708/2/89)

VAT: Construction: VAT certificates for residential or charity buildings (708/4/89)

Land and property (Notice 742 — April 1989)

Figure 28 — Bristol Visual and Environmental Buildings Trust's "Over the Shop" project (see Appendix C) is helping to improve West Street, Old Market, Bristol. The AHF loaned £50,000 in 1988 towards the cost of stripping out, restoring and upgrading this early 18th century property.

Figure 29 — Even Grade I buildings fall on hard times. Kettlethorpe Hall in Wakefield, West Yorkshire, was savagely vandalised before Yorkshire BPT started work in 1989 to restore the fabric and convert the Hall into two houses, assisted by a loan of £150,000 from the AHF.

Limited relief

Limited relief is available in the form of zero-rating for "approved alterations" (ie those that require and receive listed building consent) to "protected" buildings (ie listed buildings and scheduled monuments). It should be noted that all repair and maintenance work is liable to VAT at the standard rate, as are any alterations done without the requisite consent. The zero-rating of approved alterations is done by the building contractor (who must therefore be "registered" for VAT) and not by the BPT.

As from 1 April 1989, it is only possible for building contractors to zero-rate approved alterations to protected buildings which would qualify for zero-rating if newly constructed. These are:

— dwellings, ie individual houses and flats;

- dwellings, ie individual houses and flats; most buildings used for community residential purposes — eg a home for children, old people or the disabled, a hospice, or student accommodation, but not a hospital, or a hotel, inn or similar establishment;
- buildings used by charities (i) other than in the course or furtherance of a business (the main beneficiaries of this relief being churches) or (ii) as a village or similar hall providing social or recreational facilities for a local community.

Approved alterations to a protected building to convert it to one of the above uses will also qualify for zero-rating.

Full relief

Full relief, enabling recovery of *all* input tax (ie all VAT incurred on a project, including that charged by professional people for their services), may be available if you yourself qualify to register for VAT (more about this below!) and intend to sell the freehold or long leasehold (over 21 years) of a protected building for one of the above qualifying uses after it has been substantially reconstructed. Unless all that remained before reconstruction took place was the shell of the building, to qualify as "substantial reconstruction" three-fifths of the total cost of the works on the project must be attributable to "approved alterations" (ie those alterations that have received listed building consent). **This is known as "the 60% test".**

For types of qualifying buildings other than individual houses and flats, a certificate of qualifying use is required before relief can be obtained.

Potential for recovery of input tax on non-domestic buildings

As from 1 April 1989, all other work done to existing buildings is liable to VAT at the standard rate of 15%, and the sale or letting of such a building would normally be treated as an "exempt" supply, on which input tax is not recoverable. However, with effect from 1 August 1989, there is an option to charge VAT at the standard rate on the sale or letting of non-domestic buildings, on a building by building basis, with a view to recovering all input tax incurred. This concession will be of use to BPTs which are registered, or could become registered, for VAT and could therefore sell on or let non-domestic protected buildings to people who are themselves registered and able to reclaim the VAT

Figure 30 — *Still holding the record for the largest revolving fund project: a view of one of the terraces of Railway Cottages, Derby, before rehabilitation.*

Figure 31 — *Railway Cottages in 1982, transformed by Derbyshire Historic Buildings Trust (see p. 13, and figs. 11 and 25). The AHF made its largest ever loan — £250,000 — for this £1.25 million project.*

Figure 32 — *Kirklees Historic Buildings Trust took on these derelict Victorian cottages in a suburb of Huddersfield, West Yorkshire, as a first project in 1988. See also fig 42.*

Figure 33 — *The AHF supported Kirklees HBT by lending £27,000 for 2-3 Newhouse Place, Highfields.*

charged on the transaction. It should be noted, however, that the BPT will have to exercise the option to tax in advance of sale in order to be able to reclaim VAT on the building's rehabilitation; and that once the option has been made for that building it is irrevocable, so that VAT must be charged on sale whether or not the buyer is VAT-registered and able to reclaim.

Registration for VAT

Registration is mandatory for any "person" (an all-embracing term that includes a charity or limited company) who makes taxable supplies of goods or services in the course of a business:

— **at any time** if there are reasonable grounds for believing that future taxable turnover (not just profit) will exceed a specified amount (currently £23,600) in the year then beginning; or
— **at the end of any calendar year** if past taxable turnover exceeded a specified amount (currently £8,000) in that quarter or a specified amount (currently £23,600) in the last four quarters.

If taxable turnover is below these limits, you may nonetheless apply for registration if you can show that it would be to your advantage.

In the case of a revolving fund trust, the relevant business activity to qualify for registration is the sale or letting of a substantially reconstructed protected building (which is zero-rated); or the sale or letting of a non-domestic building (which may be standard-rated). Any other sale would be exempt, making the BPT itself "partly exempt".

Not as bad as it sounds!

Having read this far, an embryonic trust may well be feeling rather daunted. Take heart, however, from the experience of those BPTs which have already gone through the process of registering and collectively feel that it has been worth the effort. In the words of one experienced trust:

"We have been registered for VAT since before undertaking our first project, and the relatively modest amount of additional paperwork has been justified."

Indeed, the savings to be achieved can run into thousands of pounds and make all the difference to the viability of a project. This is therefore just the moment for a new trust to make use of the network of existing BPTs by asking the Association of Preservation Trusts or your APT area co-ordinator (whose name and address the Architectural Heritage Fund will provide on request) for a contact with practical experience of the registration procedure, who can advise on the advantages to be derived and any pitfalls to be avoided.

The VAT position on each individual rehabilitation project will need to be negotiated with the local VAT officer. As a general principle, be sure to keep accurate records of all accounts paid and a photographic record of the actual work as it progresses. Periodic reports (VAT returns) will have to be made to HM Customs & Excise in order to reclaim VAT where appropriate, and it is worth noting that BPTs have found that repayments can be arranged on a monthly as well as a quarterly basis.

If you plan to use a computer, you must ensure that you can still account for VAT properly and that the VAT officer can still carry out his checks. Your local VAT office will advise on how best to meet your VAT requirements *before* you commit yourself to a computer program.

Keep up to date

The above information has been checked with HM Customs & Excise, reflects the liability changes contained in the 1989 Finance Bill, and is accurate at the time of writing. Readers are, however, reminded that the guidance given may be subject to change at some later date. Those proposing to set up a new trust should therefore not neglect to consult their local VAT officer at an early stage, and ensure that they keep abreast of any changes in legislation thereafter.

Rosemary Watt.

Figure 34 — *Cainscross Toll House on the outskirts of Stroud in Gloucestershire became redundant in 1877. It suffered various changes of use before being boarded up in the 1970s.*

Figure 35 — *The property was rescued by Stroud Preservation Trust in 1988 and turned into a house. The AHF loaned £45,000.*

CHAPTER EIGHT

FUND RAISING

Some people relish the challenge of raising funds for a worthwhile cause; others dread the whole business. Whether or not your trust is fortunate enough to number among its officers or members someone with the appetite and aptitude for fund raising, it is an aspect of trust management which cannot be neglected or ducked. The trust's success in carrying out projects will indeed be largely determined by the energy and initiative it puts into mobilising the necessary cash.

One cautionary word: when preparing fund-raising materials, the trust should bear in mind that money received in response to appeals may only be applied for the particular purposes stated in the literature. It will be prudent therefore, while focusing for example on the building which is the trust's current preservation project, to include in the literature references to the need for money for future projects etc.

Start-up finance

It is generally much easier to raise money for a particular project than for the trust in general. The support of local companies, charitable trusts, private individuals, schools, clubs and other organisations is almost always more forthcoming if it can be directed towards a tangible, visible target. The trust does not have to wait, therefore, until it has raised a substantial capital sum before looking for its first project, though there is equally no reason to refrain from fund raising until a project is found.

Local authorities are under severe and increasing financial pressure, but many may be willing to provide preservation trusts with some inaugural working capital — particularly if the trust has been formed at the initiative of, or in close co-operation with, a district, town, borough or county council. The ability of local authorities to help trusts financially, as well as in other ways, underlines the importance of talking to officials and councillors at the earliest possible stage, in order to establish a relationship of confidence, mutual respect and understanding.

Professionals and publications

Whether or not local authority finance is available before a project is selected, the trust is bound to have to raise money from other sources. There is an immense volume of literature about fund raising, and a large number of people eager to sell their services, by undertaking either to raise money on other people's behalf or to teach them the techniques.

Trusts are advised not to be dazzled or daunted by the claims of fund-raising professionals, whose services they are unlikely to be able to afford. Of all the literature on the subject, that produced by the Directory of Social Change is at least as good as any, and tailored to suit various needs.[1] But although specific techniques can be learned and applied, there is no infallible prescription to follow, and no real substitute for exploring every opening and exploiting every contact trust members may have. Begging letters, to local firms and grant-giving trusts, will produce some kind of response, roughly on a 30:1 failure to success ratio. Personal approaches by trust members to company chairmen and others may prove more cost-effective. "Events" can be mounted by any and every trust member who has the energy and initiative to do so — provided that fund-raising does not become a virtually full-time preoccupation and end in itself, leaving little capacity for finding and organising a project.

Local fund raising

The trust should therefore invest a modest sum in putting together some materials to accompany letters etc — principally photographs of the building in its dilapidated condition, and small-scale reproductions of the architect's drawings of how it will look once restored. A trust member might write a short article about the trust and its proposed first project. If possible, some of this material should be combined into leaflet or broadsheet form — not lavishly, but equally not so shoddily that the photographs are blurred and the text grubby. The local paper should be persuaded to publish a feature article. Clubs, schools and businesses might be asked to display the leaflet or broadsheet, and if they would be prepared to let a trust member come to give a talk about the project.

Statutory and official finance

The prototype first project described in Appendix A, in which a preservation trust buys and restores a listed residential building in a conservation area, will be eligible for grant from both English Heritage and the local authority, and for a low-interest loan from the Architectural Heritage Fund. As these are the most commonly available sources of finance for projects undertaken by buildings preservation trusts in England, details are given below. Different types of project, involving for example the preservation and conversion of former textile mills and/or agricultural buildings, could be eligible for grants from a number of other sources.

---

[1] The Directory of Social Change, Radius Works, Back Lane, London NW3 1HL. See also Appendix H.

How to apply for grants

Prospective applicants should not rely on published information about grants and low-interest loans. Changes are frequently made to the terms and conditions governing existing sources of finance; new sources are introduced; previous sources stopped. Having identified the agencies most likely to be relevant to their projects, the trust should obtain from each details of its current programme and an application form.

Before submitting an application, the trust should ensure that it has understood and can comply with the conditions governing that particular grant or loan, and that it has included all the information required. As English Heritage's *Directory of Public Sources of Grants for the Repair and Conversion of Historic Buildings* states:

> **"Vigilance is the key to success in making applications for aid ... Always leave plenty of time for grant applications. Remember that some agencies have strict annual timetables for assessing applications and a submission at the wrong time can mean long delays or rejection. Your application is one of many and the assessment process may necessitate reference to several individuals — all with full in-trays. Before starting on the course to an application, find out about the assessment process and its timing and make allowances for holidays, etc."[1]**

If in doubt, telephone or write to the agency before filling in the application form, in order to obtain clarification of exactly what is required, and by when.

---

[1] *Directory of Public Sources of Grants for the Repair and Conversion of Historic Buildings*, available for £4 from English Heritage, Publications Department, Room 235, Fortress House, 23 Savile Row, London W1X 2HE (telephone 01-973 3000).

Information about sources of finance
England

The best quick reference work to consult about possible sources of finance for projects in England is the *Directory* published by English Heritage and referred to above. Its purpose is to provide sufficient information for prospective applicants to assess whether or not their projects may be eligible for assistance from one or more of the following:

> Department of the Environment
> Local Authorities
> English Heritage (the Historic Buildings and Monuments Commission for England)
> Development Commission/Council for Small Industries in Rural Areas
> Housing Corporation
> European Economic Community
> Department of Trade and Industry
> Ministry of Agriculture, Fisheries and Food
> Manpower Services Commission
> Sports Council
> English Tourist Board
> Architectural Heritage Fund
> Crafts Council.

As a general rule, all grants must be sought and an offer obtained and accepted before work begins, although permission can be given to start work in certain circumstances before a grant offer is confirmed. BPTs will almost certainly have to submit the budget for the project, so that grant-givers can look at the total costs involved, the estimated resale value and likely grant contributions from other sources. Grant is usually paid out either in instalments while the project is in progress or in a lump sum at the end, when the work for which it was offered has been completed to the grant-making authority's satisfaction.

English Heritage grants

There are three principal categories of English Heritage grant for BPT-type projects.

Grants to Outstanding Buildings (Section 3A grants)

English Heritage can grant aid buildings of outstanding architectural or historic interest. This usually means buildings listed Grade I or Grade II*. But occasionally closer investigation reveals something outstanding about Grade II or even unlisted buildings. Section 3A grant is normally at the rate of 40% of the cost of major repairs to the historic structure of the buildings; routine repairs and maintenance do not qualify.

Cases are individually assessed and trusts should allow up to 6 months for the development of an agreed schedule of works before a grant is offered.

Grant is paid in arrears, usually against the architect's certificates.

Contact: Historic Buildings Division, English Heritage, Fortress House, 23 Savile Row, London W1X 2HE (telephone 01-973 3000).

Grants to buildings in Conservation Areas (Section 10 grants)

Projects undertaken by BPTs will often qualify for grants offered by English Heritage under the Town and Country Planning (Amendment) Act 1972 (Section 10), normally at the rate of 25% of structural repairs to the fabric of listed and unlisted buildings in conservation areas. Higher rates of up to 50% can be considered in exceptional cases. Applications should be for buildings in conservation areas where:

— the local authority has been invited by English Heritage to submit a programme of conservation work; or
— there is a Town Scheme in operation; or
— the grant is for a scheme of conservation work prepared by a local authority, an amenity society or a group of private owners, or when one building of particular interest can be the catalyst for further action in the locality.

Figure 36 — *The medieval Chantry is the oldest building in Bridport, Dorset. Listed Grade II*, it was taken on in 1985 by the Vivat Trust, a national revolving fund which specialises in finding new uses for problem buildings.*

Figure 37 — *Vivat Trust converted the top two floors of the Chantry for holiday accommodation. The ground floor is used by the local Civic Society.*

Applications can also be made for **"buildings at risk"** grants where the building is in very poor condition and has been vacant for some time. New purchasers are not normally eligible but in appropriate circumstances this rule can be waived for buildings preservation trusts.

Section 10 grant applications are considered when full details have been provided and an inspection has been made, and grant is paid in arrears, in stages if required.

Contact: Historic Areas Division, English Heritage, 25 Savile Row, London W1X 2BT (telephone 01-973 3000).

Acquisition grants

English Heritage can make two kinds of grant for the acquisition of historic buildings which are clearly at risk.

Section 5B of the Historic Buildings and Ancient Monuments Act 1953 enables English Heritage to offer local authorities grants of up to 25% of the purchase price of buildings of special architectural or historic interest. Local authorities may then sell the building to a preservation trusts.

English Heritage can also give Section 10 grants for acquisition where a buildings preservation trust will be undertaking repairs, if acquisition will make a significant contribution towards preserving or enhancing the character of a conservation area. Section 10 acquisition grants are generally restricted to buildings preservation trusts operating a revolving fund. The normal rate of grant is 25% of the cost of repairs and purchase combined.

Contact: Historic Buildings Division, English Heritage, 25 Savile Row, London W1X 2BT (telephone 01-973 3000).

London grants

The Local Government Act 1985 empowers English Heritage to offer grants for up to 50% of the cost of repair work to enhance and protect the architectural interest and maintain the historic features of listed buildings in the Greater London area. Routine maintenance work is not eligible.

Contact: English Heritage, London Division, London Grants Section, Chesham House, 30 Warwick Street, London W1R 6AB (telephone 01-973 3000).

Conditions attached to English Heritage grants

English Heritage grants are offered subject to the condition that the recipient may be required to repay part or all of the grant if the project makes a profit. This condition has tended not to be enforced in the case of buildings preservation trusts.

Local Authority grants (England and Wales)

Local authority grants in England and Wales, like grants from English Heritage, must be applied for and accepted before work begins. They are usually paid in two or three instalments as work proceeds. If work for which the grant was offered is not completed to the local authority's satisfaction, the recipient can be required to repay.

Grants or loans for repair or maintenance of historic buildings

The Local Authorities (Historic Buildings) Act 1962 as amended by Section 58 of the Town and Country Planning Act 1968 empowers local authorities, both counties and districts, to offer grant, normally up to a maximum of 50% of estimated costs, for the repair and maintenance of listed buildings. This facility may be extended to cover garden areas attached to such buildings, and to buildings of historic or architectural interest that are not listed.

Contact: local authority.

Home Improvement Grant

NB The terms and conditions of all the grants described under this heading will change following the completion of its passage through Parliament early in 1990 of the Local Government and Housing Bill. The broad principles should however remain much the same. Charities are exempt from the requirement in the Bill to provide an owner's certificate and/or to submit to a means test when applying for "Renovation" grants (the new umbrella term for the grants described below), and from the requirement to repay if the building is sold within a certain period.

The Local Authority Housing Act 1985 (which will be superseded by the Local Government and Housing Bill) empowers local authorities to offer grants to improve residential buildings:

> **Intermediate grants** (for basic improvements and associated repairs).
>
> Local authorities must offer grants of up to 75% of the cost of installing standard missing amenities (eg bath or shower, hand-basin, sink, hot-and cold-water supply, water closet).
>
> **Improvement grants** (for major improvements and for providing homes by conversion).
>
> Local authorities have discretion to offer grant of up to 50% of the costs of substantial structural repair to houses in a poor condition. The grant may also cover the cost of conversion work to provide more housing (eg by dividing a house into two or more flats).
>
> **Repairs grants**
>
> Local authorities have discretion to offer grant of up to 75% for substantial and structural repairs to

pre-1919 houses below a certain rateable value. Works which qualify for a repairs grant are, for example, works to the roof, walls, floors or foundations. Routine maintenance work like re-wiring or replacement of worn fixtures (such as baths) will not qualify.

If a local authority is not making discretionary grants, a trust should ask it to declare the property unfit for human habitation. It would then qualify for a mandatory Intermediate grant.

Grants for Community Centres

Local authority education departments can offer grants for converting disused historic buildings into community centres, whether or not the scheme also provides tourist or entertainment facilities. 25% of costs will be provided by the local authority, 25% by the Department of Education and Science, and 50% must be raised by the community group.

Contact: local authority.

Scotland

The best source of published information for trusts undertaking projects in Scotland is *Sources of Financial Help for Scotland's Historic Buildings*, published by the Scottish Civic Trust on behalf of the Historic Buildings and Monuments Directorate. Trusts should also get in touch with:

> Historic Buildings Division
> Historic Buildings and Monuments
> Scottish Development Department
> 20 Brandon Street
> Edinburgh EH3 5RA.
> Telephone 031-244 2946.

> Scottish Civic Trust
> 24 George Square
> Glasgow G2 1EF.
> Telephone 041-221 1466.

Grants are available under the Housing (Scotland) Act 1987 for work to bring houses up to the "tolerable" standard or to rectify fundamental defects in the structure, eg to insert a damp-proof course. Grants may also be available for conversion of existing houses or other buildings into modern housing accommodation. Details will be found in a booklet *Improve Your Home with a Grant*, available from local authorities.

Wales

Historic buildings grant in Wales is administered by:

> CADW — Welsh Historic Monuments
> Brunel House
> 2 Fitzalan Road
> Cardiff CF2 1UY.
> Telephone 0222-465511

Local authority grant in Wales is available on the same conditions as in England.

Northern Ireland

Information about grants in Northern Ireland should be sought as follows:

Historic buildings grants
NI Historic Buildings Grant Fund
Historic Monuments and Buildings Branch
Calvert House
23 Castle Place
Belfast BT1 1FY

Improvement and Repair Grants
NI Housing Executive
Housing Advice Centre
2 Adelaide Street
Belfast BT2 8GA

Housing Corporation equivalent
Housing Associations Branch
Department of the Environment
for Northern Ireland
Stormont
Belfast BT4 3SS

Architectural Heritage Fund loans

The Architectural Heritage Fund, an independent national charity, offers cheap working capital to buildings preservation trusts and other organisations with charitable status for up to 50% (subject to an upper limit of £175,000) of the gross estimated costs of any project which involves the purchase and restoration or the conversion of a historic building for its preservation. A revolving fund trust is entitled to apply for up to 65% of the estimated cost of its first project. Routine maintenance and repairs to buildings already in charitable ownership and use are not eligible.

Security

Borrowers must be able to provide security for the loan in the form either of a first charge (mortgage) on the building (if it is to be sold after rehabilitation) or a written guarantee of repayment from a bank, local authority or comparable corporate body.

Timetable

Applications to the Architectural Heritage Fund are considered quarterly, normally in March, June, September and December. Loans are usually offered for two years, and interest at 5% per annum is payable when the capital is repaid.

Payment

Money from the Architectural Heritage Fund is advanced as soon as the legal formalities are complete. If the loan is secured by a first charge, the initial advance is followed by staged payments based on the project's cash flow programme and justified by architects' certificates, and the capital must be repaid as soon as the property, or any part of it, has been sold. If the loan is secured by a repayment guarantee, it is paid in a single lump sum and may be retained for two years.

Contact: The Administrator, The Architectural Heritage Fund, 17 Carlton House Terrace, London SW1Y 5AW (telephone 01-925 0199).

Figure 38 — *In 1989 British Historic Buildings Trust started restoring Cwmdows, an early 17th century farmhouse in Newbridge, Gwent. The AHF is lending £45,000.*

Figure 39 — *A former pub and adjoining Grade II listed building in Bury St Edmunds, Suffolk, were empty for several years before being recommissioned as two houses by Bury St Edmunds Town Trust, to which the AHF loaned £35,000 in 1987.*

Figure 40 — *Hatton Castle, near Newtyle in Angus, was built in 1575 by the fourth Lord Oliphant. It stood roofless and ruinous for two-and-a-half centuries before being gifted to the Hatton Castle Trust, formed by a member of the Oliphant clan.*

Figure 41 — *In 1987 the AHF loaned £50,000 towards the cost of restoring and reconstructing Hatton Castle as a clan museum.*

Appendices

A PROTOTYPE FIRST PROJECT

Many trusts are formed in response to local concern about a particular building, and their first project gets under way at the same time as the trust itself. Where this is not the case, a newly-formed trust would be well advised to look for something relatively modest on which to cut its teeth and begin to establish a track record. A first project probably should not encompass radical conversion, although it could involve division of a single unit into two or more, reintegration of multiple units into a single dwelling, or modification from residential to commercial (shop or office) use or vice versa.

The prototype described here is modelled on a real first project, though names and various details have been changed. The location is "Broadburn", a large industrial town in the north of England. The trust, called "Weston & District Buildings Preservation Trust", was formed at the joint initiative of Broadburn Borough Council and the local civic society.

The property

Weston & District Buildings Preservation Trust's first project is 6 and 7 East Hill, Broadburn Heights, Weston, a pair of semi-detached, two storey, mid-19th century, stone-built houses on a principal approach road to Broadburn. The property is in the Broadburn Heights conservation area. One of the pair is listed Grade II; the other is unlisted.

The genesis of the project

Once a favoured Victorian suburb, Broadburn Heights went downhill between the wars. Numbers 6 and 7 East Hill suffered from multi-occupation and neglect, before being compulsorily purchased in the mid-1970s, together with a number of other properties in Broadburn Heights, to make way for a ring-road link. The road scheme was successfully opposed at appeal by residents of Weston, backed by Broadburn Civic Society. After several years of indecision, the Borough

Figure 42 — *Nos. 2 & 3 Newhouse Place, Highfields, Huddersfield, West Yorkshire, before rehabilitation by Kirklees Historic Buildings Trust in 1989 (see also figs. 32 and 33).*

Council decided to sell the properties it owned in Broadburn Heights, but their appalling condition and the depressed state of the local economy made buyers reluctant to come forward. The Borough planning officer recommended that the Council itself should restore one or two of the houses in the hope of inspiring confidence in the potential of the area and encouraging private purchasers, but the money to do this could not be found. The planning officer then approached the Civic Society (which had expressed concern about the run down condition of Broadburn Heights), with the result that a trust was formed in order to undertake, as its first project, the exemplary rehabilitation of one pair of houses.

Broadburn Borough Council has therefore agreed to sell 6 and 7 East Hill to Weston & District Buildings Preservation Trust at the property's full current value (to be determined by the District Valuer), but to treat all but 10% of the purchase price as an interest-free loan to be repaid by the Trust from sales proceeds.

The work to be done

Nos 6 and 7 East Hill are empty and boarded up. Both have been damaged by vandals. They are chronically damp, afflicted by woodworm and patches of wet rot, and wholly unmodernised. Rehabilitation work includes clearance of accumulated debris, demolition of rear extensions, repairs to the basic fabric, re-roofing, damp coursing, woodworm treatment, replumbing and wiring, restoration and reinstatement of period features, installation of central heating and of kitchen and bathroom fitments, and formation of a small garden area for each house with vehicle access and parking. The estimated cost of the project (including acquisition) is £82,000, and the two houses together are expected to sell for £66,000 (the estate agent estimates that No 6, with three bedrooms, will fetch £35,000 and No 7, with two bedrooms, £31,000).

Financing the project

(Sources of grant and loan finance are described in greater detail in Chapter Eight.)

English Heritage

Because one of the buildings is listed and both are in a conservation area, some of the work may well qualify for Section 10 grant from English Heritage. The usual rate for Section 10 grant is 25% of structural repairs to the fabric of the building, including restoration of features of historical or architectural interest.

Local authority

The project should be eligible for both Historic Buildings, Intermediate and Home Improvement grants from Broadburn Borough Council.[1] Historic Buildings

grants are given for up to 50% of necessary repair and maintenance (but not all local authorities give any Historic Buildings grant at all); Intermediate grants for up to 50% of the cost of structural repair work; and Home Improvement grants for up to 75% of the cost of installing standard amenities. As a charity, the trust is exempt from the requirement to repay Home Improvement grant if the building is sold after restoration.

The Architectural Heritage Fund

Because of the change of ownership, the project should qualify for a low-interest loan from the Architectural Heritage Fund. As this is a revolving fund trust's first project, the AHF will in principle be prepared to lend up to 65% of gross estimated costs, at 5% per annum (payable when the capital is repaid), for two years or until the property is sold. The AHF will also meet the legal costs it incurs in contracting the loan. (If this were the trust's second or subsequent project, the Architectural Heritage Fund would be willing to lend up to 50% of gross estimated costs, and would pass on its legal costs to the trust.)

The trust's bank

The budget shows how the books should balance at the end of the day, forecasting that the project should at least break even (see below). It does not however show when and where the cash will come from to pay each bill submitted. In order to calculate both the

---

[1] See Chapter Eight. Intermediate and Home Improvement grants will still be available, but under a different name and different conditions, once the Local Government and Housing Bill becomes law in 1990.

overall bank borrowing requirement, and the phasing of income and expenditure, the budget must be translated into a cash flow statement (see below). This reveals that there will be an imbalance between expenditure and income at certain moments as work proceeds. The trust will therefore need to arrange in advance to be able to borrow up to £10,000 from its bank, offering a second charge on the property as security.

Fund raising

Both the budget and the cash flow statement err on the side of optimism, assuming that the properties can be turned round in nine months, that grants will be paid promptly, in instalments, as work proceeds, and that there will be no unexpected extra costs. Much could happen to distort these projections. The margin between profit and loss is moreover very fine. Weston & District Buildings Preservation Trust will therefore need to try to raise money from other sources to provide a cushion against delays, unforeseen problems, and/or a disappointing sale price.

The Trust should not set its fund-raising target at the relatively modest sum required to cushion this project. Instead, it should aim for £10,000, focusing the campaign on 6 and 7 Broadburn Heights (which is and long has been a visible eyesore), but taking every opportunity also to publicise the Trust in general, so that if the project does more than break even the Trust will have accumulated a useful amount of working capital for future projects.

THE BUDGET

The budget for the project sets out estimated income and expenditure vertically, like this:

Expenditure

	£	£
Acquisition	15,000	
Insurance	200	
Rehabilitation work	48,850	
Architect's fees and expenses (including feasibility study)	5,750	
Surveyor's fees	850	
Legal fees	275	
Building inspection	350	
Landscaping and planting	500	
Estate agent	1,500	
VAT	9,000	
Miscellaneous/contingency	5,000	
Sub-total	87,275	
Loan repayments		
AHF	52,000	
Bank	10,000	
Interest on loans*		
AHF @ 5%	1,073	
Bank @ 17%	497	
Sub-total	63,570	
Total expenditure		150,845

Income

	£	£
Loans:		
AHF	52,000	
Bank	10,000	
Grants:		
Local Authority:		
Intermediate	3,000	
Improvement	10,000	
Historic buildings	2,250	
English Heritage	10,300	
Sale	66,000	
Total income		153,550

* This assumes that the trust will be able to repay loans in less than 12 months.

CASH FLOW STATEMENT FOR 6 AND 7 EAST HILL, BROADBURN HEIGHTS, WESTON

The cash flow statement allocates income and expenditure from the budget according to the timetable for the project, as follows:

	April	May	June	July	August	Sept	Oct	Nov	Dec	Total
Expenditure										
Purchase of Property	1,500								13,500	15,000
Architect's Fees		2,750	1,000		1,000		1,000			5,750
Surveyor's Fees		850								850
Insurance	200									200
Builder's Costs		730	6,450	9,100	12,335	15,000	5,235			48,850
Building Inspection	350									350
Landscaping									500	500
Loan Repayments: AHF									52,000	52,000
Bank									10,000	10,000
Interest on Loans									1,570	1,570
Legal Fees	200								75	275
Estate Agent's Fees									1,500	1,500
VAT			3,000	2,000	1,000	1,000	2,000			9,000
Misc and Contingency	250	250	250	500	500	500	750	750	1,250	5,000
TOTAL	2,500	4,580	10,750	11,600	14,835	16,500	8,985	1,250	79,895	150,845
Income										
Loans:										
AHF	17,000			7,000	9,000	12,000	7,000			52,000
Bank		5,000						5,000		10,000
Grant:										
Local Authority (improvement)					6,500			6,500		13,000
English Heritage				5,000				5,300		10,300
Historic Building				2,250						2,250
Resale of Property								6,600	59,400	66,000
TOTAL	17,000		5,000	14,250	15,500	12,000	7,000	23,400	59,400	153,550
ACCUMULATED BALANCE	14,500	9,920	4,220	6,890	7,535	3,035	1,050	23,200	2,705	2,705
Accumulating interest on loans (payable when capital repaid)										
AHF (5%)		71	71	71	100	138	188	217	217	1,073
Bank (17%)				71	71	71	71	71	142	497

THE STATUTORY LISTING SYSTEM AND CONSERVATION AREAS

The Listing System

The Secretary of State for the Environment, and the Secretaries of State for Scotland and Northern Ireland, are required to compile lists of buildings in England and Wales of special architectural or historic interest, for the guidance of local planning authorities. Buildings that qualify for the list are:

England and Wales

— all buildings before 1700 which survive in anything like their original condition;
— most buildings between 1700 and 1840, though selection is necessary;
— between 1840 and 1914, buildings of definite quality and character, the selection being designed to include the principal works of the principal architects. Selected buildings of 1914 to 1939 are also considered.

In choosing buildings, particular attention is paid to:
— special value within certain types, either for architectural or planning reasons or as illustrating social and economic history;
— technological innovation or virtuosity;
— group value, especially as examples of town planning;
— association with well-known characters or events.

Scotland

All buildings erected before 1840, the character of which remains substantially unimpaired, are included on the list. Later buildings are selected on the basis of their individual character and quality. Special regard is paid to:
— planned streets, villages or burghs;
— works of well known architects;
— buildings associated with famous people or events;
— good examples of buildings connected with social and industrial history and the development of communications;
— distinctive regional variations in design and use of materials;
— good examples within individual building types;
— technological innovation.

Northern Ireland

Criteria similar to those for England are applied when deciding which buildings of architectural or historic interest should be listed.

Grades of listed building

England and Wales

Grade I. Buildings of exceptional interest (fewer than 5% of listed buildings are Grade I).

Grade II. Buildings of special interest. Some particularly important buildings in Grade II are classified as Grade II*.

Scotland

Category A. Buildings of national or more than local importance, either architectural or historic, or fine, little-altered examples of some particular period, style or type.

Category B. Buildings of primarily local importance, or good examples of some period, style or type which may have been altered.

Category C(S). Good buildings which may be considerably altered but retain elements of interest; and simple, often traditional buildings which group well with others in categories A and B or are part of a planned group such as an estate or an industrial complex.

Northern Ireland

Category A. Buildings of outstanding or exceptional merit and importance, which may not be destroyed.

Category B. Buildings which it is desirable to retain. Some buildings are graded B+.

Grades in Northern Ireland are not published. Owners are informed only that their building is listed.

Conservation areas

The concept of **conservation areas** originated, in England, in the Civic Amenities Act 1967, a private member's Bill introduced by Duncan Sandys (founder and then President of the Civic Trust). This recognised that as well as individual buildings of particular historic or other interest, there were whole areas of special architectural or historic interest, the character of which it was desirable to preserve or enhance. Four conservation areas were designated in 1967, and by 1988 there were more than 6,000 in England alone.

Statutory protection for conservation areas was first provided in England in the Town and Country Planning Act 1971, which placed upon local authorities the duty to pay special attention to the desirability of preserving their character or appearance and required extra publicity to be given to planning applications affecting conservation areas. Additional protection was provided by the 1974 Town and Country Amenities Act, which gave planning authorities control over the demolition of all unlisted buildings in conservation areas (except listed buildings, for which listed building consent is required; ecclesiastical buildings in ecclesiastical use; scheduled monuments, for which scheduled monument consent is needed; and buildings in one of the exempted categories set out in DOE and Welsh Offices circulars 8/87 and 61/81 respectively).

Planning authorities are able to impose additional controls in conservation areas by making an "Article 4 direction". When such a direction is in operation, express planning permission must be sought for specified types of development — such as alterations to gates, walls and fences; erection of garages, sheds, porches and storage tanks; and even external paintwork — which would otherwise be "permitted development". Article 4 directions affecting unlisted buildings must be approved or confirmed by the Secretary of State.

A very similar system operates in Scotland and Northern Ireland.

Sources of information

England

The complete *List of Buildings of Special Architectural or Historic Interest* is held by the Department of the Environment, Listing Branch (HSD2), Lambeth Bridge House, London SE1 7SB. Every local authority holds lists of buildings in its area. These are open to the public.

Conservation area policy is dealt with by HSD3 at the same address as the DOE Listing Branch.

Wales

Lists are held by Cadw — Welsh Historic Monuments, Brunel House, 2 Fitzalan Road, Cardiff CF2 1UY, and by local authorities as above.

Scotland

Lists are held by Historic Buildings and Monuments Directorate, Scottish Development Department, 20 Brandon Street, Edinburgh EH3 5RA. See also the Department's publication, *Scotland's Listed Buildings : A Guide to their Protection* (1988).

Northern Ireland

Lists are held by the Historic Buildings and Monuments Branch, Department of the Environment, Belfast, and by local authorities.

APPENDIX C

ENGLISH HERITAGE'S "BUILDINGS AT RISK" INITIATIVE AND YORK UNIVERSITY'S "OVER THE SHOP" PROJECT

"Buildings at Risk" initiative

In 1989 English Heritage introduced three new measures to help save buildings at risk: the compilation of "risk registers"; detailed guidance on temporary "holding" repairs; and grants for emergency repairs to unoccupied listed buildings.

Buildings at Risk Register

English Heritage's "risk register" is to be compiled from systematic surveys carried out by local authorities. To ensure maximum objectivity and standardisation, English Heritage has developed a piece of computer software which calculates the risk category of each building on the basis of simple data recorded by the person undertaking the survey. The results of each local authority's survey will be tabulated by English Heritage, which in due course should be able to categorise buildings at risk throughout England by geographical area, building type, age, Grade, etc. Buildings preservation trusts may be able to assist with this work and should contact the local planning authority if they are willing to do so.

Advice

To assist local authorities and owners faced with the problem of unoccupied historic buildings, English Heritage has published a book by Eleanor Michell, *Emergency Repairs for Historic Buildings*, which gives practical advice illustrated by case studies (see Bibliography).

Grants

English Heritage is now able to offer grants to help owners of listed buildings which are seriously at risk, where these buildings are of outstanding importance or situated in a conservation area. Buildings in very poor condition will be eligible for grant, normally at 25% of the cost of eligible works such as roof repairs or making the building safe. If an owner is unable or unwilling to act, the local planning authority may use its powers (under Section 101 of the Town and Country Planning Act as amended) to enter the site and carry out urgent works. Provided the extent of the works was previously agreed, English Heritage may offer grant to the local authority to cover up to 50% of any costs it is subsequently unable to recover from the owner.

Further information is available from:
   Vanessa Brand
   Conservation Officer for Buildings at Risk
   English Heritage
   25 Savile Row
   London W1X 2BT
   Telephone 01-973 3816/7

"Over the Shop" project

Vacant upper floors in traditional town centre properties present a major threat to historic buildings. Although many organisations concerned with housing are aware of the potential offered by over-the-shop accommodation, most are wary of entering this new field. A special project, funded by the Joseph Rowntree Memorial Trust, was launched in April 1989 with the aim of focusing attention on the serious conservation problems arising from the under-use of such accommodation and helping local authorities and others to do something to reverse the trend. Called "Living Over the Shop", the project is based at the Institute of Advanced Architectural Studies at the University of York.

Buildings preservation trusts, especially those which claim to have difficulty finding a building to restore, should take every opportunity to carry out an exemplary over-the-shop project, in order to demonstrate the social, commercial and conservation benefits of rehabilitating mixed use properties and encourage the private sector, housing associations and others to replicate their success.

Further information is available from:
   "Living Over the Shop"
   Project Director — Ann Petherick
   University of York
   The King's Manor
   York YO1 2EP
   Telephone 0904-656507

APPENDIX D

MODEL GOVERNING INSTRUMENT FOR A LOCAL BUILDINGS PRESERVATION TRUST

The following draft Memorandum and Articles of Association for a company "limited by guarantee and not having a share capital" are the recommended governing instrument for a local buildings preservation trust, and are an up-dated version of the Model used in the formation of the majority of such trusts in England and Wales over the last twenty years.

The Model has been revised in consultation with the Charity Commission, so that it should be possible to obtain charity registration with a minimum of formality. It is advisable to make the initial approach to the Charity Commission while the new trust's own Memorandum and Articles are still at draft stage. Organisations in or south of Gloucestershire, Oxfordshire, Buckinghamshire, Bedfordshire and East Anglia should apply to the Charity Commission's London office, St Alban's House, 57-60 Haymarket, London SW1Y 4QX (telephone 01-210 3000); organisations in Wales, and in or north of Hereford & Worcester, Warwickshire, Northamptonshire and Lincolnshire should apply to the Charity Commission's Liverpool office, Graeme House, Derby Square, Liverpool L2 7SB (telephone 051-227 3191). The model is not suitable for use in Scotland.

Draft Memorandum

THE COMPANIES ACT 1985

COMPANY LIMITED BY GUARANTEE
AND NOT HAVING A SHARE CAPITAL

MEMORANDUM OF ASSOCIATION

OF

....

....

1. The name of the Company (hereinafter called "the Trust") is..

2. The Registered Office of the Trust will be situated in ....

3. The object for which the Trust is established is as follows:

To preserve for the benefit of the townspeople of .... in the Borough [or District] of .... in the County of .... and of the nation at large, whatever of the historical, architectural and constructional heritage may exist in and around the Borough [or District] of .... aforesaid in the form of buildings (including any building as defined in Section 290(1) of the Town and Country Planning Act 1971) of particular beauty or historical, archi-

tectural or constructional interest. And in furtherance of that object but not otherwise to do all or any of the following things:

(a) To buy or otherwise acquire buildings or land or any estate or interest therein.

(b) To sell, let on lease or tenancy, exchange, mortgage or otherwise dispose of buildings or land or any interest therein subject to such covenants, conditions and restrictions as are reasonably necessary to ensure the preservation of the buildings or land.

(c) To repair, renovate, restore, rebuild and generally promote the preservation of any buildings or land.

(d) To buy or otherwise acquire furniture and other equipment for use in connection with any such buildings or land; and to sell, lease or otherwise dispose of any such furniture or equipment.

(e) To make such arrangements as are necessary to enable the public to view and enjoy any buildings (whether free or at a charge).

(f) By publishing books or pamphlets or in other appropriate manner to make known to the public the existence of buildings of particular beauty or historical, architectural or constructional interest or the features of especial interest of such buildings.

(g) To undertake or support research into the means of preserving old buildings.

(h) To raise funds by subscriptions, donations, grants, loans or otherwise for the purposes of the Trust; to invite and accept gifts of all sorts and whether *inter vivos* or by will and whether or not subject to conditions; to carry out any condition imposed on any gift which may be accepted.

(i) To constitute special charitable trusts for any particular purposes of the Trust; to act as trustee of any such special trust, whether constituted by the Trust or otherwise.

(j) To enter into and carry out contracts.

(k) To employ and remunerate staff; to employ and remunerate agents; and to make all reasonable and necessary provision for the payment of pensions and superannuation to or on behalf of employees and their widows and other dependants.

(l) To borrow money for the purposes of the Trust on such terms and on such security (if any) as may be thought fit.

(m) To invest the moneys of the Trust not immediately required for its purposes in or upon such investments, securities or property as may be thought fit, subject nevertheless to such conditions (if any) and such consents (if any) as may for the time being be imposed or required by law and subject also as hereinafter mentioned.

(n) To make planning applications, applications for consent under bye-laws or building regulations and other like applications.

(o) To establish and support or aid in the establishment and support of any charitable associations or institutions and to subscribe or guarantee money for charitable purposes in any way connected with the purposes of the Trust or calculated to further its objects.

(p) To co-operate with any local or public authority or other body concerned to achieve the object of the Trust.

(q) Generally, to do any things necessary for the attainment of the Trust's object.

Provided that:

(i) In case the Trust shall take or hold any property which may be subject to any trusts, the Trust shall only deal with or invest the same in such manner as allowed by law, having regard to such trusts.

(ii) The object of the Trust shall not extend to the regulation of relations between workers and employers or organisations of workers and organisations of employers.

(iii) In case the Trust shall take or hold any property subject to the jurisdiction of the Charity Commissioners for England and Wales, the Trust shall not sell, mortgage, charge or lease the same without such authority, approval or consent as may be required by law, and, as regards any such property, the Council of Management or Governing Body of the Trust shall be chargeable for any such property that may come into their hands and shall be answerable and accountable for their own acts, receipts, neglects and defaults, and for the due administration of such property in the same manner and to the same extent as they would have been as such Council of Management if no incorporation had been effected, and the incorporation of the Trust shall not diminish or impair any control or authority exercisable by the Chancery Division or the Charity Commissioners over such Council of Management but they shall, as regards any such property, be subject jointly and separately to such control or authority as if the Trust were not incorporated.

(iv) The Trust shall have regard at all times to the need to secure, improve or control public access to all buildings preserved by the Trust but not necessarily to the interior of such buildings of which only the exterior is of particular beauty or historical, architectural or constructional interest.

4. The income and property of the Trust whencesover derived shall be applied solely towards the promotion of the object of the Trust as set forth in this Memorandum of Association, and no portion thereof shall be paid or transferred directly or indirectly by way of dividend, bonus or otherwise howsoever by way of profit to the members of the Trust.

Provided that nothing herein shall prevent the payment, in good faith, of reasonable and proper remuneration to any officer or servant of the Trust or to any member of the Trust, in return for any services actually rendered to the Trust, nor prevent the payment of interest at a rate per annum not exceeding 2% less than the base lending rate prescribed for the time being by a clearing bank selected by the Council of Management, or at 3% per annum (whichever is the greater) on money lent, or of reasonable and proper rent for premises demised or let by any member to the Trust; but so that no member of the Council of Management shall be appointed to any salaried office of the Trust or any office of the Trust paid by fees, and that no remuneration or other benefit in money or money's worth shall be given by the Trust to any member of such Council (the Council of Management) except:

(i) repayment of out-of-pocket expenses and interest at the rate aforesaid on money lent or reasonable and proper rent for premises demised or let to the Trust.

(ii) payment in good faith to any member of the Council being a person engaged in any profession, of all usual or professional or other charges for business done and all time spent by him or his firm on behalf of the Trust when instructed by his co-members so to act in that capacity provided that such member is absent from all meetings of the

Trust during discussion of matters relevant to his remuneration for such business and does not vote on any resolutions concerning this remuneration and is not counted for the purpose of ascertaining whether or not the quorum is present at any meeting considering such a resolution.

(iii) payment of fees, remuneration or other benefit in money or money's worth to a company of which a member of the Council may be a member, and in which such member shall not hold more than one hundreth part of the capital.

5. The liability of the members is limited.

6. Every member of the Trust undertakes to contribute to the assets of the Trust, in the event of the same being wound up while he is a member, or within one year after he ceases to be a member, for payment of the debts and liabilities of the Trust contracted before he ceases to be a member, and of the costs, charges and expenses of winding up, and for the adjustment of the rights of the contributories among themselves, such amount as may be required not exceeding ....

7. If upon the winding up or dissolution of the Trust there remains, after the satisfaction of all its debts and liabilities, any property whatsoever, the same shall not be paid to or distributed among the members of the Trust but shall be given or transferred to some other charitable institution or institutions having objects which are similar to the objects of the Trust and which shall prohibit the distribution of its or their income and property among its or their members to an extent at least as great as is imposed on the Trust under or by virtue of Clause 4 hereof, such institution or institutions to be determined by the members of the Trust at or before the time of dissolution, and if and so far as effect cannot be given to such provision, then to some other charitable object.

8. True accounts shall be kept of the sums of money received and expended by the Trust and the matters in respect of which such receipts and expenditure take place, of all sales and purchases of property and goods by the Trust and of the property, credits and liabilities of the Trust, and subject to any reasonable restrictions as to the time and manner of inspecting the same that may be imposed in accordance with the regulations of the Trust for the time being, such accounts shall be open to the inspection of the members. Once at least in every year the accounts of the Trust shall be examined and the correctness of the income and expenditure account and balance sheet ascertained by one or more properly qualified Auditor or Auditors.

Draft Articles of Association

THE COMPANIES ACT 1985

COMPANY LIMITED BY GUARANTEE
AND NOT HAVING A SHARE CAPITAL

ARTICLES OF ASSOCIATION

OF

....

....

GENERAL

1. In these presents the words standing in the first column of the Table next hereinafter contained shall bear the meanings set opposite to them respectively in the second column thereof, if not inconsistent with the subject or context:

WORDS	MEANINGS
The Act	The Companies Act 1985
These Presents	These Articles of Association and the regulations of .... from time to time in force.
The Trust	The above named ....
The Council	The Council of Management for the time being of the Trust.
The Office	The registered office of the Trust.
Seal	The Common Seal of the Trust.
Month	Calendar Month.
In writing	Written, printed or lithographed, or partly one and partly another, and other modes of representing or reproducing words in a visible form.

And words importing the singular number only shall include the plural number, and vice versa.

Words importing the masculine gender only shall include the feminine gender, and

Words importing persons shall include corporations.

Subject as aforesaid, any words or expressions defined in the Act or any statutory modification thereof in force at the date on which these presents become binding on the Trust shall, if not inconsistent with the subject or context, bear the same meanings in these presents.

2. The number of members with which the Trust proposes to be registered is .... but the Council may from time to time register an increase of members.

55

3. The provisions of Sections 191(7), 352 and 353 of the Act shall be observed by the Trust, and every member of the Trust shall either sign a written consent to become a member or sign the register of members on becoming a member.

4. The Trust is established for the object declared in the Memorandum of Association.

5. The subscribers to the Memorandum of Association and other such persons as the Council shall admit to membership in accordance with the provisions hereinafter contained shall be members of the Trust.

MEMBERS

6. The following persons and none others shall be members of the Trust:

(A) Such persons as subscribe to the Memorandum and Articles of Association before the registration thereof.

(B) Such other persons or corporations as may desire to be admitted to membership and who may be elected by the Council to be members of the Trust.

In these presents the expression "Corporation" shall be deemed to include any body corporate, any county, local or other public authority and any unincorporated association whom the Council may elect to membership.

7. Any election of a person to be a member of the Trust under the provisions of Article 6 Sub-Article (B) shall conform to the following regulations and conditions:

(1) Such person must be proposed for election by a member of the Council and fourteen days' notice shall be given to the members of the Council of the meeting at which it is intended to propose such person for election, stating the object of the meeting, the name and address of the person to be proposed and the name of the member of the Council proposing such person.

(2) Such person must sign and deliver to the Trust an application for admission to membership framed in such terms as the Council shall require.

In the event of such person being elected in accordance with the above regulations he shall be entered as a member of the Trust on the Register.

8. No member of the Council shall supply or be directly or indirectly interested (other than as a shareholder in a company in which the member shall hold not more than one-hundreth part of the capital or as an official of a Bank at which the Trust's funds are deposited) in the supply of work or goods to the Trust except by way of free gift or on a basis which shows no profit or gain directly or indirectly to the member concerned.

9. Any member may terminate his membership of the Trust by notice in writing served on the Trust and thereupon he shall be deemed to have resigned and his name shall be removed from the Register of members.

10. If any member shall fail in the observance of these Articles or of any regulations of the Council made under any powers vested in them or for other sufficient reason the Council may convene an Extraordinary General Meeting of the Trust for the purpose of considering an extraordinary resolution for the expulsion of such member and on such extraordinary resolution being passed the name of such member shall be removed from the Register of members, and he shall thereupon cease to be a member.

GENERAL MEETINGS

11. A general meeting of the Trust shall be held in every calendar year as its Annual General Meeting at such time (not being more than fifteen months after the holding of the last preceding General Meeting) and place as the Council shall appoint provided that so long as the Trust shall hold its first Annual General Meeting within eighteen months of its incorporation it need not hold it in the year of its incorporation or in the following year.

12. All General Meetings, other than Annual General Meetings, shall be called Extraordinary General Meetings.

13. The Council may, when they think fit, convene an Extraordinary General Meeting, and Extraordinary General Meetings shall be convened on such requisition or, in default may be convened by such requisitionists, as provided by Section 368 of the Act.

14. Subject to the provisions of Section 378(2) and (3) of the Act relating to Special Resolutions, and to the provisions of Section 369 of the Act relating to Annual General Meetings, fourteen days' notice at the least (exclusive of the day on which the notice is served or deemed to be served and of the day for which the notice is given) specifying the place, the day and the hour of meeting, and in case of special business the general nature of such business, shall be given to the members in manner hereinafter mentioned, or in such other manner (if any) as may be prescribed by the Trust in General Meeting; but with the consent of all the members entitled to receive notices thereof or of such proportion thereof as is prescribed by the Act in the case of meetings other than Annual General Meetings, a meeting may be convened by such notice as those members think fit. The accidental omission to give notice to any member, or the non-receipt by any member of such notice, shall not invalidate the proceedings at any General Meeting.

PROCEEDINGS AT GENERAL MEETINGS

15. The business of an Annual General Meeting shall be to receive and consider the accounts and balance sheets and the reports of the Council and Auditors, to elect members of the Council in place of those retiring and also additional members of the Council, and to elect Auditors and fix their remuneration. All other business transacted at an Annual General Meeting shall be deemed special.

16. No business shall be transacted at any General Meetings, except the adjournment of the meeting, unless a quorum of members is present at the time when the meeting proceeds to business, and such quorum shall consist of not less than .... members personally present.

17. If within .... from the time appointed for the meeting a quorum be not present, the meeting, if convened upon the requisition of members, shall be dissolved. In any other case it shall stand adjourned to the same day in the next week at the same time and place, and if at such adjourned meeting a quorum be not present within .... from the time appointed for the meeting, the member or members present shall be deemed to be a quorum and may do all business which a full quorum might have done.

18. The Chairman (if any) of the Council, or in his absence the Vice-Chairman (if any) shall preside as Chairman at every General Meeting of the Trust. If there be no such Chairman, or if at any meeting he be not present within .... after the time appointed for holding the meeting, the members present shall choose one of the members of the Council present to be Chairman, or if no member of the Council be present and willing to take the Chair, the members present shall choose one of their number to be Chairman.

19. The Chairman may, with the consent of any meeting at which a quorum is present (and shall if so directed by the meeting) adjourn the meeting from time to time and from place to place, but no business shall be transacted at any adjourned meeting other than the business left unfinished at the meeting from which the adjournment took place. When a meeting is adjourned for twenty-one days or more, notice of the adjourned meeting shall be given as in the case of an original meeting. Save as aforesaid, it shall not be necessary to give any notice of an adjournment or of the business to be transacted at an adjourned meeting.

20. At any General Meeting a resolution put to the vote of the meeting shall be decided on a show of hands unless a poll is, before or upon the declaration of the result of the show of hands, demanded by the Chairman or by at least .... members present in person or by proxy, or by a member or members present in person or by proxy and representing one-tenth of the total voting rights of all the members having the right to vote at the meeting, and unless a poll be so demanded, a declaration by the Chairman of the meeting that a resolution has been carried, or carried unanimously, or by a particular majority, or lost, or not carried by a particular majority, and an entry to that effect in the Minute Book of the Trust, shall be conclusive evidence of the fact without proof of the number or proportion of the votes recorded in favour of or against that resolution. The demand for a poll may be withdrawn.

21. Subject to the provisions of the next succeeding Article, if a poll be demanded in manner aforesaid it shall be taken at such time and place and in such manner as the Chairman of the meeting shall direct, and the result of the poll shall be deemed to be the resolution of the meeting at which the poll was demanded.

22. No poll shall be demanded on the election of a Chairman of a meeting or on any question of adjournment.

23. In the case of an equality of votes, whether on a show of hands or on a poll, the Chairman of the meeting shall be entitled to a second or casting vote.

24. The demand for a poll shall not prevent the continuance of a meeting for the transaction of any business in addition to the question on which a poll shall have been demanded.

VOTES OF MEMBERS

25. Every member shall have one vote.

26. (a) Save as herein expressly provided, no person other than a member duly registered shall be entitled to be present or to vote on any question, either personally or by proxy or as proxy for another member at any General Meeting.

(b) Any corporation which is a member of the Trust may by resolution of its governing body authorise such person as it thinks fit to act as its representative at any meeting of the Trust and the person so authorised shall be entitled to exercise the same voting powers on behalf of the corporation he represents as that corporation could have exercised if it were a personal member of the Trust. A corporation represented at a meeting by its authorised representative shall be deemed for all purposes to be present in person. A copy of the resolution appointing its representative which shall be certified as a correct copy by the Chairman or another recognised officer of the governing body of a corporation, shall be conclusive evidence of such appointment.

27. Votes may be given on a poll either personally or by proxy. On a show of hands a member present only by proxy shall have no vote, but the representative of a corporation may vote on a show of hands. A corporation may vote by its duly authorised representative appointed as provided by Article 26(b) or Section 375 of the Act. A proxy need not be a member.

28. The instrument appointing a proxy shall be in writing under the hand of the appointor or of his attorney duly authorised in writing.

29. The instrument appointing a proxy and the power of attorney (if any) under which it is signed or a notarially certified copy thereof shall be deposited at the office or at such other place within the United Kingdom as is specified for the purpose in the notice convening the meeting at least forty-eight hours before the time appointed for holding the meeting or adjourned meeting at which the person named in such

instrument proposes to vote, otherwise the instrument of proxy shall not be treated as valid. No instrument appointing a proxy shall be valid after the expiration of twelve months from the date of its execution.

30. A vote given in accordance with the terms of an instrument of proxy shall be valid notwithstanding the previous death of the principal or revocation of the proxy, provided that no intimation in writing of the death or revocation shall have been received at the office or other place as aforesaid one hour at least before the time fixed for holding the meeting.

31. Any instrument appointing a proxy shall be in the following form, or as near thereto as circumstances will admit:

....

....

"I

   of

   a member of .... (hereinafter called "the Trust") and entitled to one vote, hereby appoint

               of

   and failing him

               of

   to vote for me and on my behalf at the [Annual or Extraordinary, as the case may be] General Meeting of the Trust to be held on the .... day of .... and at any adjournment thereof.

As Witness my hand this ..... day of .... 19..."

COUNCIL OF MANAGEMENT

32. The affairs of the Trust shall be managed by the Council of Management. The number of the members of the Council shall not be less than .... nor more than.................

33. The members of the Council shall be:

   (A) The Subscribers to the Memorandum of Association and

   (B) Such other persons (being members of the Trust) as shall from time to time be elected by the Council or by the members of the Trust in General meeting.

Provided that no person who is employed by the Trust and receiving any salary, fees, remuneration or other benefit in money or money's worth from the Trust (save as permitted by clause 4 of the Memorandum of Association) shall be eligible for membership of the Council.

PROCEEDINGS OF THE COUNCIL OF MANAGEMENT

34. The Council may meet together for the dispatch of business, adjourn and otherwise regulate their meetings as they think fit, and determine the quorum necessary for the transaction of business. Unless otherwise determined .... shall be a quorum. Questions arising at any meeting shall be decided by a majority of votes. In case of an equality of votes the Chairman shall have a second or casting vote.

35. A member of the Council may, and on the request of a member of the Council the Secretary shall at any time, summon a meeting of the Council by notice served upon the several members of the Council. A member of the Council who is absent from the United Kingdom and who has no registered address in the United Kingdom shall not be entitled to notice of a meeting.

36. The Council shall from time to time elect a Chairman who shall be entitled to preside at all meetings of the Council at which he shall be present, and may determine for what period he is to hold office, but if no such Chairman be elected or if at any meeting the Chairman be not present within five minutes after the time appointed for holding the meeting and willing to preside, the members of the Council shall choose one of their number to be Chairman of the meeting.

37. A meeting of the Council at which a quorum is present shall be competent to exercise all the authorities, powers and discretions by or under the regulations of the Trust for the time being vested in the Council generally.

38. The Council may delegate any of their powers to committees consisting of such member or members of the Council as they think fit, and any committee so framed shall in the execution of the powers so delegated conform to any regulations imposed on it by the Council. The meetings and proceedings of any such committee shall be governed by the provisions of these presents for regulating the meetings and proceedings of the Council so far as applicable and so far as the same shall not be superseded by any regulations made by the Council as aforesaid. All acts and proceedings of any such committee or committees shall be reported back as soon as possible to the Council.

39. All acts *bona fide* done by any meeting of the Council or of any committee of the Council, or by any person acting as a member of the Council shall, notwithstanding it be afterwards discovered that there was some defect in the appointment or continuance in office of any such member or person acting as aforesaid or that they or any of them were disqualified, be as valid as if every person had been duly appointed or had duly continued in office and was qualified to be a member of the Council.

40. The Council shall cause proper minutes to be made of all appointments of officers made by the Council and of the proceedings of all meetings of the Trust and of the Council and of committees of the Council, and all business transacted at such meetings, and any such minutes of any meeting, if purporting to be signed by the Chairman of such meeting, or by the Chairman of the next succeeding meeting, shall be sufficient evidence without any further proof of the facts therein stated.

41. A resolution in writing signed by all the members for the time being of the Council or of any committee of the Council who are duly entitled to receive notice of a meeting of the Council or of such committee shall be as valid and effectual as if it had been passed at a meeting of the Council or of such committee duly convened and constituted.

POWERS OF THE COUNCIL

42. The management of the business and the control of the Trust shall be vested in the Council, who, in addition to the powers and authorities conferred upon them, may exercise all such powers and do all such acts and things as may be exercised or done by the Trust and are not hereby or by the Act expressly directed or required to be exercised or done by the Trust in General Meeting. At meetings of the Council, each member of the Council shall have one vote only, except that in the case of equality of votes the Chairman shall, in addition have a second or casting vote.

43. The members for the time being of the Council may act notwithstanding any vacancy in their body, provided always that if at any time the members of the Council be reduced in number below the minimum prescribed by these presents, it shall be lawful for the members available to act as the Council for the purpose of admitting persons to membership of the Trust, filling up vacancies in their body or of summoning a General Meeting but for no other purpose.

44. The Council may at any time appoint any person to be a member of the Council either to fill a casual vacancy or as an addition to the existing membership (but not so as to exceed the maximum number of members prescribed by these presents). Any person so appointed shall hold office only until the next following Annual General Meeting and shall then be eligible for re-election but shall not be taken into account in determining the number of members of the Council who are to retire by rotation at such meeting.

45. Without prejudice to the general powers conferred by Article 42 and to the other powers and authorities conferred as aforesaid, it is hereby expressly declared that the Council shall be entrusted with the following powers, namely:

PARTICULAR POWERS

(1) To pay the costs, charges and expenses preliminary and incidental to the formation and establishment of the Trust and matters incidental thereto.

(2) To purchase or otherwise acquire for the Trust any property, rights or privileges which the Trust is authorised to acquire at such price and generally on such terms and conditions as they may think fit.

(3) To raise or borrow money for the purposes of the Trust from any person, corporation or other body and, with the approval of the Charity Commissioners for England and Wales, to secure the repayment of the same together with any interest and premium thereon, by Mortgage or charge upon the whole or any part of the assets and property of the Trust, present or future, and to issue bonds, debentures, or debenture stock, either charged upon the whole or any part of the assets and property of the Trust or not so charged, and in connection therewith to take out and maintain sinking fund or redemption policies.

(4) At their discretion to pay for any property or rights acquired by or services rendered to the Trust either wholly or partially in cash or in bonds, debentures, or other securities of the Trust.

(5) With the approval aforesaid to secure the fulfilment of any contracts or engagements entered into by the Trust by Mortgage or charge of all or any of the property and rights of the Trust or in such manner as they may think fit.

(6) To appoint and at their discretion remove or suspend such officers and other staff for permanent, temporary or special services as they may from time to time think fit, and to invest them with such powers as they may think expedient, and to determine their duties and fix their salaries or emoluments, and to require security in such instances and to such amounts as they think fit.

(7) To institute, conduct, defend, compound or abandon any legal proceedings by or against the Trust or its officers or otherwise concerning the affairs of the Trust and also to compound and allow time for payment or satisfaction of any debts due and of any claims or demands by or against the Trust.

(8) To refer any claims or demands by or against the Trust to arbitration and observe and perform the awards.

(9) To make and give receipts, releases and other discharges for money payable to the Trust and for the claims and demands of the Trust.

(10) To determine who shall be entitled to sign on the Trust's behalf, bills, notes, receipts, acceptances, indorsements, cheques, releases, contracts and documents.

(11) From time to time to make all such regulations and bye-laws as they think proper with regard to the affairs and concerns of the Trust, and from time to time to repeal and alter the same or make others in lieu thereof as may seem expedient. Provided that the same do not contravene any of the provisions herein contained, and provided that no bye-laws or regulations shall be made under this power which would amount to such an addition to or modification of the Articles of Association as could only legally be made by a Special Resolution passed in accordance with the provisions of Section 378 of the Act.

ROTATION OF MEMBERS OF THE COUNCIL

46. At the first Annual General Meeting of the Trust all the members of the Council shall retire from office, and at the Annual General Meeting in every subsequent year one-third of the members of the Council for the time being, or, if their number is not three or a multiple of three, then the number nearest one-third, shall retire from office.

47. The members of the Council to retire in every year shall be those who have been longest in office since their last election, but as between persons who became members on the same day those to retire shall (unless they otherwise agree among themselves) be determined by lot.

48. A retiring member of the Council shall be eligible for re-election.

49. The Trust may, at the meeting at which a member of the Council retires in manner aforesaid, fill the vacancy by electing a person thereto, and in default the retiring member shall, if offering himself for re-election, be deemed to have been re-elected, unless at such meeting it is expressly resolved not to fill such vacancy or unless a resolution for the re-election of such member shall have been put to the meeting and lost.

50. No person other than a member of the Council retiring at the meeting shall, unless recommended by the Council, be eligible for election to membership of the Council at any general meeting unless, not less than .... nor more than .... days before the date appointed for the meeting, there shall have been left at the registered office of the Company notice in writing, signed by a member duly qualified to attend and vote at the meeting for which such notice is given, of his intention to propose such person for election, and also notice in writing signed by that person of his willingness to be elected.

51. The Trust may from time to time by ordinary resolution increase or reduce the number of members of the Council, and may also determine in what rotation the increased or reduced number is to go out of office.

52. The Trust may by ordinary resolution, of which special notice has been given in accordance with section 379 of the Act, remove any member of the Council before the expiration of his period of office notwithstanding anything in these Articles or in any agreement between the Trust and such member.

53. The Trust may by ordinary resolution appoint another person in place of a member of the Council removed from office under the immediately preceding Article. Without prejudice to the powers of the Council under Article 44 the Trust in General Meeting may appoint any person to be a member of the Council either to fill a casual vacancy or as an additional member. The person appointed to fill such a vacancy shall be subject to retirement at the same time as if he had become a member of the Council on the day on which the member in whose place he is appointed was last elected as a member.

DISQUALIFICATION OF MEMBERS OF THE COUNCIL

54. The office of a member of the Council shall be vacated:

(A) If he becomes bankrupt or insolvent or compounds with his creditors.

(B) If he becomes of unsound mind.

(C) If he be convicted of an offence the commission of which by a member of the Council could bring the Trust into disrepute.

(D) If he is requested in writing by a majority of his fellow members of the Council to resign.

(E) If he gives to the Council one month's notice in writing to the effect that he resigns his office.

(F) If he ceases to be a member by virtue of Section 293 of the Act.

55. A member of the Council who is in any way, whether directly or indirectly, interested in a contract or proposed contract, arrangement, or dealing with the Trust, shall declare the nature of his interest at a Meeting of the Council, and subject thereto and subject to the right of the remaining members of the Council to resolve that he withdraw and not vote on the particular matter, he may be counted in the quorum present at any meeting of the Council whereat such contract, arrangement or dealing with the Trust is considered or entered into and may vote in respect thereof.

SECRETARY

56. The Secretary shall be appointed by the Council on such terms as to length of service, remuneration and generally as the Council may think fit and the Council may remove any Secretary so appointed. The provisions of sections 283(1)-(3) and 284 of the Act shall be observed. The Council may from time to time appoint a deputy or assistant Secretary who may act in the place of the Secretary if there be no Secretary or no Secretary available to act or capable of acting.

THE SEAL

57. The seal of the Trust shall not be affixed to any instrument except by the express authority of a resolution of the Council or of a committee of the Council empowered thereto, and in the presence of two members of the Council and of the Secretary or such person other than the Secretary as the Council may appoint for the purpose; and such members of the Council and the Secretary or other person as aforesaid shall sign every instrument to which the seal of the Trust is so affixed in their presence, and in favour of any purchaser or person *bona fide* dealing with the Trust such signatures shall be conclusive evidence of the fact that the seal has been properly affixed.

INCOME OF THE TRUST

58. The income of the Trust shall be applied solely towards the promotion of the object of the Trust as set

forth in the Trust's Memorandum of Association as the Council may from time to time think fit (and in particular the Council shall have power to transfer all or any part of such income to trustees to be applied by them for the advancement of the object of the Trust in such manner as they shall think best) with power to the Council to create a reserve fund or reserve funds to be applicable for any such purposes, and, if the Council shall think fit, also to apply all or any part of the reserve fund appropriated to any particular purpose to any other one or more of such purposes, and, pending any such application, any reserve fund may at the discretion of the Council either be employed in the business of the Trust or be invested from time to time in such investment as the Trust may think fit.

ACCOUNTS

59. The Council shall cause accounting records to be kept in accordance with Sections 221-223 of the Act.

60. The books of account shall be kept at the office or, subject to Sections 222(1) and (2) of the Act, at such other place or places as the Council may determine, and shall always be open to the inspection of the Council. The Council may from time to time by resolution determine whether and to what extent and at what times and places and on what conditions the books and accounts of the Trust or any of them shall be open to the inspection of the members not being members of the Council, and the members shall have only such rights of inspection as are given to them by the Act or by such Resolution as aforesaid.

61. At the Annual General Meeting in every year the Council shall lay before the Trust an income and expenditure account for the period since the preceding account, or in the case of the first account since the incorporation of the Trust, made up to date not more than six months before such meeting. A balance sheet as at the date to which income and expenditure account is made up, shall be made out and laid before the trust at the Annual General Meeting. Every such balance sheet shall be accompanied by proper reports of the Council and the Auditors. A copy of every balance sheet (including every document required by law to be annexed thereto) which is to be laid before the Trust in General Meeting, together with a copy of the Auditor's report, shall, twenty-one clear days previously to such meeting, be sent to the Auditor and every member entitled to receive notices of General Meeting in the manner in which notices are hereinafter directed to be served.

AUDIT

62. Auditors shall be appointed and their duties regulated in the manner provided by Sections 236, 237, 241, 262, 384-392 and 713 of the Act, or any statutory modification thereof for the time being in force, and for this purpose the said sections shall have effect as if "member of the Council" and "the Council" were substituted for "Director" and "the Directors" respectively.

NOTICES

63. A notice may be served by the Trust upon any member either personally or by sending it through the post addressed to such member at his registered address.

64. No member shall be entitled to have a notice served on him at any address not within the United Kingdom, and any member whose registered address is not within the United Kingdom may by notice in writing require the Trust to register an address within the United Kingdom which, for the purpose of the serving of notices, shall be deemed to be his registered address. Any member not having a registered address within the United Kingdom, and not having given notice as aforesaid, shall be deemed to have received in due course any notice which shall have been displayed in the office and shall remain there for the space of forty-eight hours, and such notice shall be deemed to have been received by such member at the expiration of twenty-four hours from the time when it shall have been so first displayed.

65. Any notice if served by post shall be deemed to have been served at the expiration of twenty-four hours after the same shall have been posted, and in proving such service it shall be sufficient to prove that the envelope containing the notice was properly addressed and stamped and put into the post office or into any post box subject to the control of the Postmaster General.

DISSOLUTION

66. Clause 7 of the Memorandum of Association relating to the winding up and dissolution of the Trust shall have effect as if the provisions thereof were repeated in these Articles.

The Model Constitution is available from The Architectural Heritage Fund, 17 Carlton House Terrace, London SW1Y 5AW (telephone 01-925 0199)

A SAMPLE PROTECTIVE COVENANT

This Deed of Covenant is made the First day of April One thousand nine hundred and ninety nine between WESTON AND DISTRICT BUILDINGS PRESERVATION TRUST whose registered office is situate at 10 East Hill Broadburn Heights Weston (hereinafter called "the Trust") of the one part and JOSEPH JAMES BLOGGS of 3 Tight Fit Cold Drive Easton being the Purchaser of Number 6 East Hill Broadburn Heights Weston in the County of Oldshire and all the persons whose names are or shall hereafter be entered at the end hereof and who now or shall hereafter execute these presents (hereinafter called "the Owner") of the other part

W H E R E A S:
(1) The Trust have acquired and renovated the building known as Number 6 East Hill Broadburn Heights Weston in the County of Oldshire (hereinafter called "the said property")

(2) The Trust is desirous of selling the said property in fee simple to Joseph James Bloggs and is also desirous that so far as the law shall allow the covenants hereby entered into by Joseph James Bloggs and his successors shall be enforceable by the Trust against the owner of the said property under any doctrine of law or equity that shall be applicable at the time and whether or not the Trust shall at such time have or retain any land capable of benefiting from the performance or observance of such covenant or covenants

NOW IN CONSIDERATION of the sale of the said property to Joseph James Bloggs and to give effect to the said desires of the Trust

THIS DEED WITNESSETH as follows:
1. THE Owner in respect of the said property HEREBY COVENANTS with the Trust and with any Trust body or institution that shall at any time succeed to or otherwise take over the assets and functions of the Trust as follows:

(1) To repair and keep in repair the said property and the drains and sewers belonging to the same and making no alteration to the external appearance of the said property;

(2) To insure and keep insured the said property and appurtenances against loss or damage by fire and other risks and special perils normally insured under a comprehensive policy in a sum equal to the full value thereof with some insurance company of repute to be approved in writing by the trust and whenever and if required to produce the insurance policy or a copy thereof and the receipt for the last premium due in respect of such insurance to the Trust or its agent and in case the said property shall be destroyed or damaged by fire or such other risks and perils the money received in respect of such insurance shall be forthwith laid out in rebuilding or reinstating the same and in case the said monies shall be insufficient for that purpose the owner will make good the deficiency out of his own monies and if at any time the owner shall fail to keep insured the said property or to produce the policy of insurance and the receipt for the last premium or either of them when required as aforesaid it shall be lawful for but not obligatory on the Trust to insure the same as aforesaid and the Owner will on demand repay to the Trust all monies expended by it in such insurance and all costs and expenses in relation thereto;

(3) If at any time the Owner shall be entitled to the benefit of an insurance on the said property which is not effected or maintained in pursuance of his obligation aforesaid then all monies received by virtue of such insurance shall if the Trust so requires be laid out in making good the loss or damage in respect of which the same shall have been received;

(4) If the said property is damaged or destroyed to rebuild or reinstate the same within one year of any such damage having occurred subject to the obtaining of all statutory consents and permissions or if such consent only be given to a rebuilding or reinstatement with modifications in accordance with such modification;

(5) To permit the Trust with or without its agent workman surveyor or others to enter upon the said property at reasonable times in the daytime when considered necessary by the Trust for the purpose of inspecting the state of repair of the said property and to make good within one calendar month after notice in writing by the Trust or its agent all defects in repair then found;

(6) The Owner shall before making any transfer of the said property give notice in writing to the Trust of such intended conveyance transfer assent gift or similar deed or document stating the name and address of the person to whom the property is to be transferred and pay the proper legal costs of the Trust for registering such notice and for preparing this Deed for fresh execution;

(7) To use the said property as a shop, offices or a private dwellinghouse or a combination of such purposes only;

(8) Not without the consent of the Trust and of the Local Authority under the Town and Country Planning Acts and Building Regulations for the time being in

force and the grant of any necessary rights by adjoining owners to erect any building or structure on the said property nor to erect or make any extension or alteration to the building thereon PROVIDED THAT

(a) The Consent of the Trust shall not be required for any internal alterations or additions (including decorative) other than alterations or additions affecting

    (i) the staircase from the ground floor to the first floor

    (ii) the two nineteenth century first floor fireplaces

    (iii) all exposed stained woodwork other than woodwork forming part of a floor

(b) without derogating from the generality of this clause the consent of the Trust shall be required (but subject as hereinafter provided will not be unreasonably withheld) for the external redecoration of the property

(9) Not to use the said property or any part thereof or permit or suffer the same to be used for any illegal or immoral purposes;

(10) On any sale or other contract for the disposition of the title of the said property to stipulate in the Contract that the Purchaser or other person acquiring thereunder shall execute this Deed as an Owner and shall (if it becomes appropriate) in the instrument of Transfer apply to the Chief Land Registrar for registration of a restriction against registration of any disposition without the consent of the Trust and shall secure provisions with any chargee whereunder

(a) The obligations of this Deed shall become enforceable against a Purchaser who shall acquire an interest from the chargee pursuant to the exercise of a power for sale and

(b) A restriction in the following form shall be entered upon the Charges Register:

"Restriction registered on   Except under an Order of the Court or of the Registrar no disposition by way of sale is to be registered without the consent of Weston and District Buildings Preservation Trust of 10 East Hill Broadburn Heights Weston" and the Trust hereby agrees and declares in favour of all future purchasers and chargees that the consent referred to above shall be given PROVIDED THAT a sale is effected SUBJECT TO the provisions of this Deed secured by the execution thereof by the Purchasers;

(11) On any disposition of the title otherwise than in pursuance of a contract to require the disponee to execute this Deed and to secure registration of restrictions to the same effects as aforesaid;

(12) On any lease or other creation or disposition of a lesser interest in the said property to impose in the instrument effecting such lease or other transaction obligations which will safeguard or facilitate the observance and performance of all the above covenants;

2. THE Trust hereby reserves the right to modify waive or release any covenants restrictions or stipulations relating to any part of 6 East Hill Broadburn Heights Weston whenever imposed or entered into and the right to modify waive or release hereby reserved shall be exercisable by the Trust and those deriving title under it or any person or body to whom this right may be expressly assigned

3. IT IS HEREBY AGREED AND DECLARED as follows:

(1) The liability under the covenants herein before contained shall extend to cover the acts and omissions not only of the covenantor but of all those claiming through or under him but as soon as any new owner or owners of the respective title shall execute this Deed as such the preceding owner or owners shall thenceforth be released and discharged from any obligation thereafter to perform and observe the said covenants and from all liability in respect of breaches thereof committed or permitted thereafter but without prejudice to the continuance of liability for any breaches occurring there before

(2) The singular shall include the plural and the masculine shall include the feminine and vice versa

(3) This Deed shall be kept at the registered office of the Trust for the time being or at such other office or place as the Trust may notify in writing to the Owner and shall be kept reasonably accessible for any Owner for the time being to inspect and take copies and available for the speedy effectuation of execution hereof by any person in accordance with the terms hereof

IN WITNESS whereof the Trust has caused its Common Seal to be hereunto affixed the day and year first before written and the other parties hereto have hereunto set their respective hands and seals the days and years hereinafter respectively appearing

THE COMMON SEAL of

WESTON AND DISTRICT BUILDINGS PRESERVATION TRUST

WESTON AND DISTRICT BUILDINGS PRESERVATION TRUST

was hereunto affixed in the presence of:

Prudence Upright   Secretary

Ernest Caution   Member of the Council

SIGNED SEALED and DELIVERED
by the OWNERS
in the presence of:

NAME	DATE	SIGNATURE	SEAL	WITNESS
JOSEPH JAMES BLOGGS	8.12.89			
		JJ Bloggs		
CONSTANCE FIDELITY	9.12.89			
		Constance Fidelity		

63

ARCHITECTURAL HERITAGE FUND REGISTER
OF REVOLVING FUND PRESERVATION TRUSTS
(with year of foundation)

The Architectural Heritage Fund maintains a Register of "revolving fund" buildings preservation trusts in the United Kingdom. To qualify for entry, a trust must have charitable status, must give priority amongst its objects to the preservation of buildings for the benefit of the community, and must be constituted so that money released from one project is applied to another. At the end of November 1989 the following trusts were registered with the AHF (in alphabetical order by county):

England

Avon

Avon Industrial Buildings Trust Ltd	1980
Bath Preservation Trust	1934
Bristol Buildings Preservation Trust Ltd	1981
Bristol Visual & Environmental Buildings Trust Ltd	1982
Weston-super-Mare Trust	1984

Buckinghamshire

Amersham Historic Buildings Trust Ltd	1984
Buckinghamshire Historic Buildings Trust Ltd	1983

Cambridgeshire

Cambridge Preservation Society	1929
Cambridgeshire Cottage Improvement Society Ltd	1938
Cambridgeshire Historic Buildings Preservation Trust	1984
Ely Preservation Trust Ltd	1979

Cheshire

Chester Historic Buildings Preservation Trust Ltd	1981

Cleveland

Cleveland Buildings Preservation Trust Ltd	1982

Cornwall

Cornwall Buildings Preservation Trust Ltd	1973

Cumbria

Brampton Preservation Trust Ltd	1981
Carlisle Buildings Preservation Trust	1989
Kendal Civic Society Building Preservation Trust Ltd	1977

Derbyshire

Derbyshire Historic Buildings Trust	1974
Peak Park Trust	1987

Devonshire

Devon Historic Buildings Trust Ltd	1973
Plymouth Barbican Association Ltd	1957
Totnes & District Preservation Trust	1985

Dorset

Dorset Building Preservation Trust Co Ltd	1985

Co Durham

Teesdale Buildings Preservation Trust	1976

East Sussex

Sussex Heritage Trust Ltd	1977

Essex

Southend Building Preservation Trust Ltd	1978

Gloucestershire

Gloucester Historic Buildings Ltd	1980
Gloucestershire Heritage Trust Ltd	1984
Stroud Preservation Trust Ltd	1982

Greater London

Croydon Building Preservation Trust Ltd	1979
Environment Trust for Richmond upon Thames	1986
Hackney Historic Buildings Trust	1985
Haringey Buildings Preservation Trust	1981
Heritage of London Trust Ltd	1980
Spitalfields Historic Buildings Trust Ltd	1977

Greater Manchester

Bolton & District Building Preservation Trust	1982
Manchester Heritage Trust Ltd	1980

Hampshire

Hampshire Buildings Preservation Trust Ltd	1975
Romsey & District Buildings Preservation Trust Ltd	1975

Hereford and Worcester

County of Hereford & Worcester Building Preservation Trust Ltd	1965
City of Worcester Building Preservation Trust Ltd	1978
Herefordshire Buildings Conservation Trust Ltd	1980

Hertfordshire

Hertfordshire Building Preservation Trust Ltd	1963
Royston Buildings Preservation Trust Ltd	1981

Isle of Wight
Isle of Wight Buildings Preservation Trust Ltd   1979

Kent
Kent Building Preservation Trust   1968

Lancashire
Burnley & District Civic Trust Building
   Preservation Trust Ltd   1977
Pendle Building Preservation Trust Ltd   1976

Leicestershire
Leicestershire Historic Buildings Trust Ltd   1981

Merseyside
Liverpool Buildings Preservation Trust   1984
Merseyside Buildings Preservation Trust   1988

Norfolk
King's Lynn Preservation Trust Ltd   1959
Norfolk Historic Buildings Trust   1977
Norwich Preservation Trust Ltd   1965

North Yorkshire
North Craven Building Preservation Trust   1976
Richmondshire Preservation Trust   1978
Stokesley Buildings Preservation Trust   1979

Northamptonshire
Rothwell Preservation Trust   1985

Northumberland
Berwick-upon-Tweed Preservation Trust   1985

Nottinghamshire
Nottinghamshire Building Preservation Trust Ltd   1967

Oxfordshire
CPRE Oxfordshire Buildings Preservation
   Trust Ltd   1971
Oxfordshire Buildings Trust Ltd   1981

Shropshire
Ironbridge & Coalbrookdale Buildings
   Preservation Trust Ltd   1975
Shrewsbury Civic Society Trust Ltd   1978
Shropshire Building Preservation Trust   1985

Somerset
Frome Historic Buildings Trust Ltd   1975
Somerset Building Preservation Trust   1988
Sun Street Trust   1987

South Yorkshire
Sheffield, Rotherham & District Buildings
   Trust Ltd   1971

Staffordshire
East Staffordshire Heritage Trust   1983
Staffordshire Historic Buildings Trust   1982

Suffolk
Ipswich Building Preservation Trust Ltd   1978
Suffolk Building Preservation Trust Ltd   1973

Surrey
Farnham (Building Preservation) Trust Ltd   1968
Surrey Historic Buildings Trust Ltd   1979

Tyne and Wear
Tyne & Wear Building Preservation Trust Ltd   1979

West Midlands
West Midlands Historic Buildings Trust   1985

West Yorkshire
Kirklees Historic Buildings Trust   1984
Leeds Buildings Preservation Trust Ltd   1977
Todmorden Buildings Preservation Trust   1988

Wiltshire
Bradford-on-Avon Preservation Trust Ltd   1964
Chippenham Civic Society Trust Ltd   1985
Malmesbury Preservation Trust   1987
Melksham Town Trust   1985
Warminster Preservation Trust Ltd   1987
Wiltshire Historic Buildings Trust Ltd   1967

Regional
Northern Heritage Trust Ltd   1982
North West Buildings Preservation Trust Ltd   1982
Yorkshire Buildings Preservation Trust Ltd   1980

National
British Historic Buildings Trust   1983
Industrial Buildings Preservation Trust Ltd   1975
Vivat Trust Ltd   1981

Wales

Cardiff Building Preservation Trust   1985
Pembrokeshire Historic Buildings Trust   1985
West Glamorgan Buildings Trust   1984

Scotland

Alloa Tower Building Preservation Trust   1989
Bridgegate Trust Ltd   1982
Castles of Scotland Preservation Trust   1985
Cockburn Conservation Trust   1978
Highland Buildings Preservation Trust   1986
Lothian Building Preservation Trust   1983
North East Scotland Preservation Trust   1985
Scottish Historic Buildings Trust   1985
Strathclyde Building Preservation Trust   1985

Northern Ireland

Historic, Environmental & Architectural
   Rehabilitation Trust   1972

TOTAL 105 Trusts

SOME USEFUL NAMES AND ADDRESSES

Government

ENGLAND

Department of the Environment (Listing Branch)
Lambeth Bridge House
London SE1 7SB
Telephone 01-211 3000

English Heritage
Fortress House
23 Savile Row
London W1X 2HE
Telephone 01-973 3000

The Charity Commission
London Office
St Alban's House
57-60 Haymarket
London SW1Y 4QX
Telephone 01-210 3000

National, London, and services charities; charities in Bedfordshire, Buckinghamshire, Cambridgeshire, Essex, Hertfordshire, Kent, Norfolk, Suffolk, Surrey and Sussex. Registrations of charities in counties otherwise covered by the South West office.

South West Office
The Deane
Tangier
Taunton
Somerset TA1 4AY
Telephone 0823-321102

Existing charities in Avon, Berkshire, Cornwall, Devon, Dorset, Gloucestershire, Hampshire, Oxfordshire, Somerset, Wiltshire. Registrations of potential charities in these counties are dealt with in London.

Liverpool Office
Graeme House
Derby Square
Liverpool L2 7SB
Telephone 051-227 3191

Charities in all other counties of England, and all charities in Wales.

SCOTLAND

Historic Buildings and Monuments, Scottish Development Department
20 Brandon Street
Edinburgh EH3 5RA
Telephone 031-556 8400

WALES

CADW — Welsh Historic Monuments
Brunel House
2 Fitzalan Road
Cardiff CF2 1UY
Telephone 0222-465511

The Charity Commission
Graeme House
Derby Square
Liverpool L2 7SB
Telephone 051-227 3191

NORTHERN IRELAND

Historic Buildings and Monuments Branch, Department of the Environment for Northern Ireland
Parliament Buildings
Stormont
Belfast BT4 3SS
Telephone 0232-230560

Registry of Companies and Friendly Societies
IDB House
64 Chichester Street
Belfast BT1 4JX
Telephone 0232-234488
ext. 471 (Friendly Societies)
ext. 445 (Companies)

Non-Governmental Organisations

The Architectural Heritage Fund
Head Office
17 Carlton House Terrace
London SW1Y 5AW
Telephone 01-925 0199

Manchester Office (Development Officer)
Environmental Institute
Greaves School
Bolton Road
Swinton
Manchester M27 2UX
Telephone 061-794 8035

The Architectural Heritage Society of Scotland
43b Manor Place
Edinburgh EH3 7EB
Telephone 031-225 9724

Association of Preservation Trusts
C/O The Architectural Heritage Fund

BPTs can join the following committees:

South West
Avon, Cornwall, Devonshire, Dorset, Gloucestershire, Somerset, Wiltshire

South East
Bedfordshire, Berkshire, Buckinghamshire, Hampshire, Hertfordshire, Isle of Wight, Kent, London, Oxfordshire, Surrey, Sussex

East Anglia
Cambridgeshire, Essex, Lincolnshire, Norfolk, Suffolk

Midlands
Derbyshire, Herefordshire, Leicestershire, Northamptonshire, Nottinghamshire, Shropshire, Staffordshire, Warwickshire, West Midlands, Worcestershire

North West
Cheshire, Cumbria, Greater Manchester, Lancashire, Merseyside, West Yorkshire

North East
Cleveland, Co Durham, Humberside, Northumberland, North & South Yorkshire, Tyne & Wear

Scotland

Wales

Northern Ireland

Charities Aid Foundation
48 Pembury Road
Tonbridge
Kent TN9 2JD
Telephone 0732-771333

Directory of Social Change
Radius Works
Back Lane
London NW3 1HL
Telephone 01-435 8171 and 01-431 1817

SAVE Britain's Heritage
68 Battersea High Street
London SW11 3HX
Telephone 01-228 3336

Society for the Protection of Ancient Buildings (SPAB)
37 Spital Square
London E1 6DY
Telephone 01-377 1644

SELECT BIBLIOGRAPHY

Some of these titles are out of print, others are too expensive to buy. Almost all ought to be available from public libraries, and can be consulted at 17 Carlton House Terrace.

Setting up a Buildings Preservation Trust

Building Preservation Trusts, A Challenge for Scotland
Scottish Georgian Society (now the Architectural Heritage Society of Scotland) 43b Manor Place, Edinburgh EH3 7EB, 1984.

Financing the Preservation of Old Buildings
A Civic Trust Report to the Department of the Environment, 1971.
ISBN 1900849592 (out of print).

Forming a Buildings Preservation Trust
A Civic Trust Report to the Department of the Environment, 1972.
ISBN 1900849622 (out of print).

Model Governing Instrument for a Local Buildings Preservation Trust
The Architectural Heritage Fund, 17 Carlton House Terrace, London SW1Y 5AW, Revised Edition 1989.

Reviving Buildings and Communities — A Manual of Renewal
Michael Talbot, David and Charles, London, 1986.
ISBN 0715386794

Setting up a Buildings Preservation Trust
North East Civic Trust , Floor 4, MEA House, Ellison Place, Newcastle upon Tyne NE1 8XS, 1980 (out of print).

Preservation

Churches — A Question of Conversion
Ken Powell & Celia De La Hey, SAVE Britain's Heritage, 68 Battersea High Street, London SW11 3HX, 1987.
ISBN 0905978242

Conservation — A Credit Account
Michael Pearce, SAVE Britain's Heritage, 68 Battersea High Street, London SW11 3HX, 1988.
ISBN 0905978250

Emergency Repairs for Historic Buildings
Eleanor Michell, English Heritage with Butterworth Architecture, English Heritage, Fortress House, 23 Savile Row, London W1X 2HE, 1989.
ISBN 1850742278

Empty Quarters — The Listed Buildings of Your Dreams
Marianne Watson-Smyth, SAVE Britain's Heritage, 68 Battersea High Street, London SW11 3HX, 1989.

A Future for Farm Buildings
Gillian Darley, SAVE Britain's Heritage, 68 Battersea High Street, London SW11 3HX, 1988.
ISBN 0905978269

Historic Buildings At Work
Scottish Civic Trust/Property Services Agency, Department of the Environment, Scotland, 1983.
ISBN 090456603X

Listed Buildings and Conservation Areas
Charles Mynors, Longman 1989.
ISBN 0851214088

Scotland's Listed Buildings : A Guide to their Protection
Historic Buildings and Monuments Directorate, Scottish Development Department, 20 Brandon Street, Edinburgh EH3 5RA, 1988.

Taken for Granted : A celebration of 10 years of Historic Buildings Conservation, including *The Repair and Maintenance of Historic Buildings: A Brief Guide for Owners, Architects and Agents*
by Richard Pierce, Alastair Coey and Richard Oram, The Royal Society of Ulster Architects and The Northern Ireland Historic Buildings Council, Belfast, 1984.
ISBN 0903058022

What Listing Means: A Guide for Owners and Occupiers
Department of the Environment (Listing Branch), Lambeth Bridge House, London SE1 7SB

Charities: The Legal Framework

A Guide to the Benefits of Charitable Status
Michael Norton, Directory of Social Change, Radius Works, Back Lane, London NW3 1HL, 1988.
ISBN 0907164269

Legal Structures for Voluntary Organisations
John Edginton and Susan Bates, National Council for Voluntary Organisations, 26 Bedford Square, London WC1B 3HU, 1984.
ISBN 0719911168

Fund Raising

Directory of Grant-Making Trusts
Charities Aid Foundation, 48 Pembury Road, Tonbridge, Kent, 1989.
ISBN 0904757404

Directory of Grant-Making Trusts and Organisations in Scotland
Scottish Council for Community and Voluntary Organisations, 18-19 Claremont Crescent, Edinburgh EH7 4QD.
ISBN 0903589834

Directory of Public Sources of Grants for the Repair & Conversion of Historic Buildings
English Heritage, 25 Savile Row, London W1X 2BT, 1988.
ISBN 1850741808

Government Grants, A Guide for Voluntary Organisations
Maggie Jones, Bedford Square Press, London 1989.
ISBN 0719912474

A Guide to the Major Trusts
Directory of Social Change, Radius Works, Back Lane, London NW3 1HL, 1989.
ISBN 0907164366

Raising Money from Industry
Directory of Social Change, Radius Works, Back Lane, London NW3 1HL, 1989.
ISBN 0907164420

Sources of Financial Help for Scotland's Historic Buildings
Scottish Civic Trust on behalf of Historic Buildings and Monuments Directorate, The Scottish Development Department, March 1989. (Available from Scottish Civic Trust, 24 George Square, Glasgow G2 1EF.)

List of Photographs

Figure 43 — *Nos. 79-80 High Street, Gravesend, Kent, after rehabilitation by Kent Building Preservation Trust in 1989 (see also fig. 22).*